SHIFTING
INTO
HIGH GEAR

Praise for
Shifting into High Gear

"Striving to be our best possible self while living with medical challenges is something I know a lot about, and when I see that drive reflected in others, like Kyle Bryant, I can't help but cheer them on. *Shifting into High Gear* chronicles a true American hero who teaches us that even when the stakes are high or bad days are upon us, those of us given this mixed blessing of pain and purpose simply have no other choice but to keep moving forward. I consider this book a gift for those of us who empathize from our own health challenges as well as anyone interested in making the most of every moment of their lives. Ride on, Kyle!"

—Montel Williams

"Kyle's disease and the odyssey he undertakes are decidedly rare, but the power of *Shifting into High Gear* is in how it relates to the personal journey of each one of us. We see our doubts in Kyle's doubts, our fears in his fears, and we see a road map for our own lives in his voyage across America. This book reminds us to take control of our reaction to the things beyond our control, of the importance of building a strong community, and that the failures in our journeys aren't what define them. With each turn of his pedals, Kyle inspires, educates, and empowers."

—Drew Dudley,
Author of *This Is Day One: A Practical Guide*
to Leadership That Matters

"Powerful. Raw. Eye-opening. Humbling. Inspiring. Kyle is courageous, smart, witty at times, and honest in his words. He represents a journey that millions of advocates are on yet whose stories haven't yet been heard. A must-read."

—Nicole Boice,
Founder/CEO Global Genes–Allies in RARE Disease

"Kyle takes us here on the ride of his life—and a ride for his life and so many others. His journey across this great country shows us all how to live without limitations. It launches Kyle into what is now his life's work and passion. We are blessed to have Kyle and his team fighting for all people with rare diseases."

—John F. Crowley,
Chairman and CEO Amicus Therapeutics

"Kyle's story is an inspiration, not just to rare disease patients, but to anyone struggling through adversity. While Friedreich's ataxia is a devastating disease, Kyle has shown that perseverance, along with support from family, friends, and the rare-disease community, can help to overcome any obstacle. People like Kyle are the reason we need to do more with the science we already have and bring life-saving treatments to millions of people suffering from rare diseases."

—Emil D. Kakkis, M.D., Ph.D.,
Founder, EveryLife Foundation for Rare
Diseases, President/CEO, Ultragenyx

"Kyle Bryant challenges us not only to aim high, dream big, and be of service to the world, but also to reconsider how we regard people—ourselves or others—who have physical abilities that differ from the norm. When a remarkable individual chooses not to be a victim of his condition, but instead to show what is possible, he makes us all understand that we are capable of more than we believe. I am honored to have played a small part in Kyle's story, and applaud him for paying it forward. *Shifting into High Gear* is truly an inspiration."

—Roz Savage, Environmental Activist,
2010 *National Geographic* Adventurer of the Year,
First Woman to Row Solo Across the
Atlantic, Pacific and Indian Oceans

"Kyle's remarkable story reflects the courage and determination that has enabled him to deal with his disease. He explores in particular the virtues of a strong rare disease community that brings patients and physicians together in a common cause. His story is a must read for anyone facing adversity."

—Peter L. Saltonstall, President and CEO,
National Organization for Rare Disorders (NORD)

SHIFTING INTO HIGH GEAR

KYLE BRYANT
WITH ALEX SCHNITZLER

Health Communications, Inc.
Deerfield Beach, Florida

www.hcibooks.com

Library of Congress Cataloging-in-Publication Data
is available through the Library of Congress

© 2019 Kyle Bryant

ISBN-13: 978-07573-2152-8 (Paperback)
ISBN-10: 07573-2152-6 (Paperback)
ISBN-13: 978-07573-2153-5 (ePub)
ISBN-10: 07573-2153-4 (ePub)

Publisher: Health Communications, Inc.
        3201 S.W. 15th Street
        Deerfield Beach, FL 33442–8190

Cover design by Kele Dobrinski
Front cover photo by VFC Inc.
Author photo by Rick Guidotti for Positive Exposure
TEAM FARA photo by Blake Andrews for SLOtography
Interior design and formatting by Lawna Patterson Oldfield

CONTENTS

For the FA Community
with appreciation for our collective story

AN AUTOBIOGRAPHY
OF STITCHES

On Monday, when I was seven, I caught my toe on a strand of barbed wire behind my grandmother's house in Oroville, California.

My cousins and I foraged along the creek with our nets, searching for anything living or crawling near the water—crawdads, frogs, lizards, water bugs. We jumped rocks and scaled gullies. The scent of the hills intoxicated us, tall dry grass, miles of uninterrupted forest. Beyond the pine trees lay the foothills of the Sierra Nevada mountain range, which stretched for hundreds of miles.

Bears lived there.

A wild frontier created the backdrop to my world. The wilderness called me, and a visit to grandma's house always promised adventure.

This day, I tried to climb over a barbed wire fence to get back to the house. My balance was awkward, and my shoelace caught on a barb. I went headfirst into a rock. Hard.

Grandma came running when she heard us screaming.

My grandma, Gladys Lacativo, had superhuman strength. She reached over the fence and plucked me from the ground. We raced to the hospital. I watched the pine trees flash above the car, and wondered if I'd get a day off from school.

DAMAGE: 10 STITCHES.

On Tuesday, when I was eleven, I tried to cut open a golf ball with a pocketknife. It's one of those stupid things you do when you're eleven.

That day, the summer sun warmed the canyons off Highway 49, a few miles from Grass Valley, California. My brother and I learned things on our quiet suburban street—how to ride a bike, how to build friendships, how to torture ants with a magnifying glass. We lived in the Lake of the Pines housing development, which surrounded a small manmade lake. We learned to golf on a course cut into the nearby terrain.

I was sitting on the tailgate of my dad's truck in our driveway when I spied a golf ball that had fallen out of someone's bag.

As an official member of the Boy Scouts of America, I owned a standard issue Boy Scout pocketknife. It was a utilitarian tool, and I was the curious type. I thought, "Let's see what's inside a golf ball."

In hindsight, a table saw would have been more appropriate, especially after the knife slipped and sliced my index finger.

My parents said, "You don't need stitches." We taped it up. No golf or baseball for weeks. A little death, but I got past it.

DAMAGE: HURT PRIDE, EXTREME BOREDOM, AN INCH-LONG SCAR TWENTY-FIVE YEARS LATER.

On Wednesday, when I was twelve, my friend Geoff's cow escaped from his pasture. This was no ordinary cow. I'm talking an award-winning cow that had recently earned a 4H blue ribbon at the county fair.

So, when the fence broke and the cow escaped, it was a big deal. Geoff's dad sent us out with some tools to fix the fence.

We ran under the basketball hoop and across uneven ground. We looped around the pond, darted between the oak trees, and past the barking dogs. Geoff's little brother trailed behind, but I was the one struggling to keep up. When we reached the pasture, we found the broken spot in the fence, a gap exactly the size of an award-winning cow.

After mending the fence, Geoff and I found a giant rock to steady the post. As we hefted the rock against the post, I stumbled and dropped the rock on my finger.

Blood flow varies from cut to cut. This gash was a slow, seeping kind, and it colored the dirt red.

DAMAGE: SIX STITCHES

Whether I ran across a pasture, negotiated uneven terrain or collected rocks to stabilize a fence post, I'd become conscious of an invisible force. I couldn't name it. I didn't understand it. Some days it felt like a hand coming out of the sky, smashing me to the ground. Other times it felt like a wind pushing from the opposite direction. My body was losing its center of gravity, and my lack of coordination grew more pronounced.

I tried to dismiss the regularity of mishaps, and my friends followed my lead. We concentrated on the activities in front of

us, not what held us back. But we suspected there was more to
the story.

On Thursday, when I was thirteen, I stood on my snowboard
at Soda Springs ski hill, near Lake Tahoe. We were on a trip with
my middle school. My mom even chaperoned. I rode the bus with
twenty other kids ready to hit the slopes.

I had reached that stage of puberty when acting cool overshadowed everything. I needed to prove myself as an athlete. The
popular guys could run faster, jump higher, and ski faster than
everyone else. I wanted to be one of those guys. I tried to "game"
our social system by riding a snowboard rather than skis because
snowboarding was more popular than skiing at the time.

I wanted to be cool.

When I got situated on the slope, I strapped into my snowboard, stood up, and took off. The invisible force slammed into me.
My reaction time was slower than most. I couldn't recalculate the
direction of my fall.

I hit the ground in total confusion.

Not cool.

When you're thirteen, and your body betrays you, a rage builds.
I cursed the mountain and the trees; I cursed my snowboard, and
the snow itself. There was a sharp pain in my wrist. The nurse
said it was a common accident, but there was nothing common
about it.

DAMAGE: BROKEN WRIST.

On Friday, when I was fourteen, during our next annual ski trip at Soda Springs, a brilliant sun turned a perfect day into a bitter one.

Crisp snow blanketed the slopes, and my best friend Andy and I were carving down the mountain.

Snow weighed down the pine boughs, and clouds of fresh powder spilled into the creeks and over ledges. I navigated behind Andy, unsteady with my speed of descent, and I lurched off-center. I tried to ignore the opposition of the invisible force, but I couldn't resist it.

After a sharp turn, the front edge of my board snagged. I went face-first into a patch of snow. My body stuck in the powder, my legs arched behind me as my board slammed into the back of my head.

DAMAGE: TEN STITCHES.

On Saturday, when I was sixteen, I demanded more from myself. I pushed myself. I tried out for every athletic team. I joined the high school volleyball team, and we traveled to UC Davis to participate in a regional tournament. The entire team was pumped and ready to win.

After a close win against one of the many teams, we raced with our sack lunches to our team's spot in the stadium seating. Other teams filled the seats below.

I ran down the stadium steps. That's what sixteen-year-olds do. They run. I was so eager to find my seat with the team, I disregarded the invisible force that was now an aggressive presence in my life.

I tripped on one of the bleacher steps. That giant hand came down and threw me headfirst into the arm of the outside chair.

I couldn't believe the amount of blood. This was one of those fast gushes.

My entire team gathered around as my coach and my dad situated me in a seat with a T-shirt to slow the blood. I walked to the car with my dad and he kept me awake as we navigated to another hospital.

DAMAGE: SIX STITCHES ABOVE MY RIGHT EYE.

On Sunday, my mom called the doctor.

CHAPTER 1

I'm the Guy
Wearing Handcuffs

Let's put it this way: When you're seventeen and you stumble like you're drunk, something's wrong.

I didn't know it was coming. For several years, my physical abilities had been declining.

Big time.

At first, the signs were small. When I grabbed a pen to take notes for class, the handwriting didn't look like mine. I would toss a ball up to catch it, and it landed in the grass. When I walked downstairs, I had to concentrate on not falling over the railing.

Soon, navigating a sidewalk became a challenge. I'd grab onto anything for support—the edge of a table, a bush, or the shoulder of a stranger.

I'd struggle to get a key in a lock, pour a glass of milk, or carry a cup of water into the living room. The spilled drink, the broken glass, and missing the keyhole were adding up. I was turning into an old man at seventeen.

The doctors ran tests, asked questions, and caused my family to orbit around an unknown that threw everything into question: What was happening?

After a year of visits to various doctors, neurologists, and finally the UCLA Ataxia clinic, my genetic material got sent to a lab. The results said I had Friedreich's ataxia (FA), a degenerative neuromuscular disease, which is most often diagnosed in children between the ages of five and fifteen.

When the doctor explained the results, the medical terminology sounded like a foreign language, but I understood enough.

I understood the invisible force that had pulled on me for years. I understood all the times I couldn't make the baseball team, stumbled during band practice, fell over on my bicycle, or couldn't leap over the railing when I was a lifeguard. I tuned into my anger, my despair, and the growing mistrust of my body when I couldn't perform simple tasks.

But when the doctor said it *shortened life expectancy*, my world burned.

This wasn't my reality.

I lived in a small Northern California town, at the base of the Sierra Nevada mountains. My reality was defined by the song I played in the car—the windows rolled down as I turned into my high school parking lot, perhaps thinking about how I was going to get beer that weekend, or how I should leave the bleach in my hair longer next time to achieve a more translucent look. I was confident, athletic, the high school prom king.

The facts of this new identity contaminated my existence. I faced a continuum that I could not change.

I thought, "You're going to hit bottom, dude."

I was going to die.

CRAWL BEFORE YOU CAN WALK

Imagine walking down a city street.

Your feet feel ten times heavier. Rather than walk, you stumble. You're crossing deep sand, wearing a tight bodysuit that restricts every movement. Maybe your vision shakes a bit, like you're experiencing sudden earthquakes with each step. At unexpected moments, your balance throws you off. Add these symptoms up and you have the onset of FA.

The optimal body corrects quickly, which allows most of us to walk and maintain balance. With a neurological disease, that correction happens slowly. They call it *loss of proprioception* and it's a hallmark of FA. Functional proprioception allows us to sense our body parts in space without looking. We can close our eyes and feel the wind, listen to the sounds around us, and remain standing.

But people with FA lose that capacity. With FA, if you close your eyes, you hit the ground. Your body loses a clear relationship to gravity.

Now, keep walking down that sidewalk. You're grateful for any patch of grass on the horizon. You're thinking, "Man, if I fall, I'm falling right there. Oh, there's a tree. I can stabilize myself. Sweet, I'm coming up to a railing. Here's a bench. Let's sit down."

That's a lot for a seventeen-year-old to handle—or anyone, at any age.

That's why on a Friday night, after leaving a college party, I was the guy who ended up sitting on the curb, wearing handcuffs.

I lived in Davis, California, at the time—twenty-one and embracing college life at the University of California. I planned to major in engineering, graduate, and get a decent job.

The party was loud, typical, and roaring drunk with twenty-somethings. When I left the house to make my careful crawl back home, the cops arrived and saw a young man stumbling down the sidewalk. Remember, I'm the guy wearing a super-tight-full-body-denim-suit-strapped-in-with-rubber bands, gravity pulling on me in unpredictable ways.

The policeman pointed to the curb. "Sit," he commanded.

I plopped.

I glared at the suburban Davis neighborhood. Davis is one of those towns in California where most of the soccer moms have PhDs. Modest single-story homes lined the streets, tidy lawns, Volvos parked in the two-car garages.

The Central Valley blew hot against my back and the entire suburban community conspired to rise against me—the students standing on their front porch, the neighbor walking his dog, the stout officer leaning over me on the curb.

I shut down and refused to communicate. The cops wouldn't believe me, anyway. They're not going to listen to a "drunk" college kid.

I could have defused the situation by addressing it head-on, but it was easier to feel victimized. It was easier to be pissed. I wanted to lash out, hurt someone. I felt sorry for myself, and I wanted to draw attention to that fact.

"Screw you!" I ranted. "You don't care about me. You don't know what's going on."

My buddy Sean tried to stand up for me. "My friend has a condition that causes him to wobble." But that was useless.

The policeman didn't try to keep the smirk off his face. To him, I was so drunk that it was a medical emergency. Pretty soon, a fire truck arrived, paramedics, more police, more flashing red lights.

All for me.

I understood the dubious look on the officer's face. Why would he even know?

Friedreich's ataxia is an unknown disease. It affects one in 50,000 people, making it officially a "rare" disease. In the U.S., the National Institutes of Health classifies a disease as rare if it has a population of less than 200,000, and FA only affects roughly 5,000 in the U.S.

But rare diseases are hardly rare. Look across the American landscape, and you'll find more than 30 million people—10 percent of the population—facing the unknown of a rare disease. It's a shadow that moves in many directions.

Eventually, things got sorted out and the cops drove me home. But, for me, things were just getting started. Why should I have expected a policeman to know about my illness? I barely understood the disease myself.

Most affected people don't want to look at disease. They don't want to witness their own finite existence stumbling down a city street, wheeling through a grocery store, or eating through a tube.

That was me.

American culture is built upon a pull-yourself-up-by-the-boot-straps mentality. We're a "do-it-yourself" society. You hear people say, "I'm grateful for my health." They often mean, "I'm glad I'm not disabled."

That's the lens through which I saw myself. I experienced my youth as an "able-bodied" person, and I had all the preconceptions —and ignorance—about disabilities. I would see a kid in a wheel-chair and think, "Oh, poor thing."

We are wired to view "difference" as a deficit. I had a vision of myself as a functional person, and it wasn't someone with a neuro-logical disease. My vision and my reality were starting to diverge.

No matter how well intentioned, liberal-minded, or compas-sionate we behave, we fault people who are not able-bodied. Even when we extend compassion toward someone's physical state, we identify their inability to operate within a "functional" range. Our range. A comfortable framework. In that moment, we place our-selves at odds with other human beings who simply want to do their thing.

I perpetuated this thinking.

One would think that when I became a young man with a dis-ability, I would gain some perspective—embrace an alternative view.

But I was slow to change.

I started to see myself as flawed, a liability. How could I provide for myself, or for a future family? How could I build a career when I couldn't walk? How could I face challenges as I became more dependent upon others?

After my diagnosis, I walked around in a fog. This wasn't happening.

I was ashamed that I might hold my friends back. I was ashamed that I might give up when things got difficult. I was ashamed that I was the weak link in my family, worried that my parents would have to care for me for the rest of my life. I didn't want anyone feeling sorry for me.

We all have a vision for our lives. That includes everyone around us. We want our moms and dads and brothers and sisters and friends to be happy, sometimes more than ourselves. As my disease cast its long shadow, someone had to take the blame. After all, it's *my* disease. Why should I limit the dreams and hopes of others?

When the policeman told me to sit on the curb, my only solution was to push back. My shame became the reason to make my push, even though it was a destructive force.

OKAY, IT'S IMPOSSIBLE,
SO LET'S BEGIN

Many see disease as an obstacle to living a formidable life. Perhaps that's the underlying shadow to all illness. Disease reminds us of our limitations, our fears, as if *disability* means the end.

This message says *Don't overextend yourself*. Don't push beyond your edge. Be wise and, above all, live in moderation.

Without a doubt, moderation is safe. Most of us *want* to feel safe. We keep our lives limited, and make sure not to overdo. Most of us barely touch our potential because we buy into this thinking.

We play a little golf, swim a little, work a little, play some cards, shoot some pool, write occasionally, or play guitar sometimes.

We all want to be well-rounded people doing everything in moderation.

However, there are a few people who get really good at something. Often these people are viewed as having unhealthy obsessions. But these are the people who excel and achieve great things.

Think the Wright Brothers; the first person to scale Mount Everest; the first man on the moon; the first woman to swim the English Channel...

Philippe Petit, the man who walked a tightrope strung across the span of the World Trade Center, was obsessed with the impossibility of his feat. In the documentary about his stunt, *Man on Wire*, he refers to this impossibility, over and over, until he says, "And slowly I thought: Okay, it's impossible. That's sure. So, let's start working."

This is a powerful concept.

When we accept the understanding that the fruits of possibility and the limits of impossibility are closely aligned, we can make the choice to move ahead, knowing the risk.

We need more obsessive people in this world—individuals who run straight toward their fear, and lean beyond their limits. If you want to pursue a dream, then you abandon your list of "what ifs" and make a risky decision.

Reaching for extremes, however, has the potential for extreme failure, and this fear often prevents us from moving forward. That's moderation, when you accept the conditions of your fate without argument.

We can all change the direction of our lives. But we must be willing to take an objective look at what's standing in the way. I wasn't willing.

My journey toward self-acceptance was not a straight line. I didn't want to do the work. I didn't want to see my disease. I struggled to redraw the boundaries of my life with my limited set of perceptions. I thought I was defective, a half-rated human body, and I clung to this belief like a pit bull.

A LOVE STORY ENDS IN AFRICA

When it came to the topic of love, for example, I was a complete disaster zone. How could I love when I'm disabled?

So, when I blundered into my college relationship with Abby Hoskins, I found out. I leapt in front of a semitruck (metaphorically). I figured what the hell. I'm a twenty-year-old kid. Seize the day. There she appeared: blond, blue-eyed, and bubbling over with life. I couldn't lose. My friends looked at me sideways every time I started raving about her. They mumbled into their coats, *What's going on with Kyle? Dude's got tunnel vision.*

Abby proved to be quite the bodyguard. She almost knocked out a guy at the next college party for insulting me. A romantic gesture—if you consider punching romantic—that initiated an unraveling of sorts, just as we were getting started.

We wandered through the party, a maze of dark hallways in the sprawling suburban home, college kids standing and leaning against walls, mad laughter, a classic college gathering in a red-plastic-cup-keg-in-the-backyard sort of way. Students littered the backyard with biting voices. Clusters of guys knocked back shots of tequila in the kitchen.

When we left, I grabbed Abby's hand and we stepped onto the front porch, where we squeezed past a tall, blond guy. The wind blew the scent of freshly cut grass into the open door. Just then, the blond guy called at Abby.

"You're going home with him? He walks like a faggot."

Abby stopped. For a split second she debated whether to let it go or react. She walked back up to the guy and he smiled. He probably thought, *Hey, I got her attention. Maybe this is going to be good for me.* So, he was caught off-guard when Abby's fist crashed into his jaw. He doubled over and grabbed his face, checking for blood and lost teeth.

Inside, I cheered. Here was a woman who not only stuck up for me, but also defended the honor of an entire demographic of individuals. Bottom line: Her reaction was badass. Of course, in my typical self-destructive fashion, I seized upon the opportunity to feel sorry for myself.

It kicked in as I grabbed her hand and pulled her away, even while he was still hunched over.

"I don't need you to stick up for me," I blurted on the way up the driveway.

That wasn't what she expected.

"What the hell are you taking about?" she said, suddenly defensive. "There was so much wrong with that comment. What am I supposed to do?"

"Well, I could have handled it," I said. That wasn't true. I knew there was no way I could have handled it, but I wouldn't admit it. I would have made a fool of myself and gotten my butt kicked.

I was pissed, but my real anger was about not being able to take care of myself. I felt like I needed to respond like a man, all macho. Instead, I was insecure.

I resented the fact that my girlfriend was doing the punching instead of me. I staggered toward home, heart pounding, fists clenched. The moment triggered a nerve. It introduced a buried notion that ate through the final months of our relationship.

No matter how much I tried to ignore my disease, it touched every aspect of my life. I couldn't separate myself. How could I embrace intimacy as an "impaired" man? Who says "forever" to a man in a wheelchair? How could a partner live with a guy who eventually won't be able to feed himself?

Considering those uncertainties, I struggled to lock in something that promised certainty. My pursuit of Abby was a sweet college crush, for sure, but during the process, I created a perfect set of working blinders. After all, I came to the relationship thinking that my disease was a flaw, and I couldn't remove myself from that perception.

That semester, Abby finished her final year of college. After graduation, she volunteered at an orphanage in Ghana, Africa, arranging her assignment through the humanitarian organization, Ananda Marga, which had established deep relationships with the communities in the North Tongu District in the Volta region. Abby wanted to become a positive force in the world, and this adventure was a first chance.

She had always talked about leaving. "It's going to suck when we have to break up," she said. I would get pissed off and frustrated and sulk around for a few days, but I supported her adventure. I thought of the scene in John Steinbeck's *Of Mice and Men*, where Lenny is holding onto the mouse—he doesn't want to let go, he loves it so much. He squeezes the mouse so hard that it dies. I was no Lenny and I wanted Abby to thrive, but I didn't really want to let go.

I couldn't stave off the inevitable, but I traveled to Africa to visit Abby for three weeks. She took time off from the orphanage in the capital city of Accra and we traveled into the countryside to visit the Mafi-Zongo Water Project, managed by Ananda Marga. They worked with local leaders to provide safe water to the outlying communities. As a young engineer-in-training, part of my focus was on water treatment, so I was interested.

We traveled with a monk who was dressed in bright orange robes. He had a long white beard, and impressed me with his careful vocabulary and thoughtful reflections. He also loved listening to Brittany Spears.

We took a bus from the city, watching as the savanna swept past the open windows, and where windswept bluffs thrust out of the earth. My imagination was activated and I saw the shadows of baboons crossing along the road, and elephants wandering through the bush. The journey to the village was interrupted when one wheel fell off our bus. We spent the next hour trying to find the lug nuts on the highway. Eventually, we recovered three of them, enough to partially secure the wheel and travel on.

When we arrived at the village, the night was black. There was no electricity here. Torches flickered against the small huts. We were led to the center of the village. People noticed my lurching gait and someone offered me a seat near the middle of the gathering.

A group of men pounded on drums while a team of girls danced to the rhythm, flapping their arms and dipping their heads. One girl would move to the center of the circle, exaggerating her movements while the villagers clapped and sang. Abby stood next to me as I nodded my head to the beat.

I knew my life was changing. I knew our relationship was ending, but it was impossible to let go. I imagined a family with children and a house with a white picket fence. I knew a wheelchair was a few years away, and I wanted to realize my vision of normalcy.

Later that evening we lay in our hut with its dirt floor and mosquito netting draped over the bed. We stared up at the roof. Footsteps ran past, slapping on the damp ground, while children laughed from a nearby hut.

"You go see the world and make a difference," I said. "I need to build my profession and learn how to sustain myself. My disease is only going to get worse, and I don't want to hold you back."

These thoughts didn't surprise her. As I frequently affirmed, I believed my options were limited, while hers seemed endless. This worldview angered me and created distance.

The nagging issue had finally come to a head.

"Well, if that's the way you feel," Abby said, "maybe we should do something about it." It confirmed that we were drifting apart.

I stood abruptly and stumbled outside to take a shower. Someone from the village brought a bucket of rainwater. A sponge floated in the center with a bar of soap. I walked into an outside stall with three walls and looked up at the stars. I realized a blond, twenty-two-year-old girl wasn't going to justify my life, but I needed something from her that I couldn't provide for myself. I saw myself as damaged and not worthy of a relationship with such a driven, attractive, and confident woman.

Perhaps if I could have owned my disability, owned my short-comings, maybe the relationship would have turned out differently. Maybe Abby wouldn't have seemed so godly.

I hadn't yet learned how to separate myself from my disability, and as I moved on with my life, this belief was taking a toll.

COMPASSION IS A TWO-WAY STREET

Not long after I returned from Africa and finished college, I applied for an *accessible* parking placard. This alone was tough. I was not only recovering from a broken heart, but it was one of those checkpoints that forced me to accept the forward momentum of my disability.

When the placard came in the mail, I opened it slowly. It read PERMANENT.

"No, you must have made a mistake," I said aloud to the walls of my apartment. "I am not going to need this forever."

"This isn't me."

At the time I spent much of my day in a luxurious cubicle at my post-college job, working as an engineer at a firm with outstanding people. Every month, I got a fat paycheck. I had great benefits, a 401(k), a big deal for a twenty-four-year-old.

But I wasn't happy. I struggled to get out of bed each day. I didn't feel particularly capable as an engineer. I chose engineering in school because I was okay at math and science, and I enjoyed getting an exact answer to a problem. I worked hard in college, but I still graduated with a 2.4 GPA. I was an average, middle-of-the-road worker bee.

I got to thinking, "Is this it? Am I supposed to settle down? Accept my fate? Live out my remaining years with resignation?"

When I was first diagnosed, there was a lot of despair in my family. While I was consumed with my own emotions—which meant I wouldn't talk to anyone about it—my family was forced to navigate the terms of a mysterious disease on their own.

One weekend, Grandma Lacativo spent the night at our house. My grandmother took my bed and I slept on the living room couch. In the morning, I lay half-awake, while my mom and grandma talked at the kitchen table. The smell of fried bacon and fresh coffee filled the house. Sunlight poured through our sliding glass doors, so I turned on my side and listened to their conversation.

My mom was explaining the disease to my grandmother, trying to outline the causes of FA and its genetic origins. She spoke in a low voice, but I listened without turning over. She described the list of symptoms—slurred speech, scoliosis, diabetes, hearing loss, vision loss, and shortened life span. She explained to my grandmother that I would reach a time when I couldn't walk, talk, swallow food…where I would be confined to a wheelchair, lose all ability to take care of myself, and eventually die.

"Kyle's genes are abnormal," my mother said.

"What do you mean, abnormal?" asked my grandma.

"Something to do with the frataxin gene," my mom said. "It produces too many repeats of a certain DNA sequence." My mother sighed, and I imagined her staring down at her hands. "I don't know," she said. "I've been trying to learn everything I can, and it looks bad. There's no cure. Nobody lives very long with this disease."

My grandmother might not have understood the language of biology, but she knew the language of compassion. She knew what this disease meant for her grandson. She understood the future that I faced.

"Well, Diane," she said after a long silence. "Kyle can have my genes. I don't need them anymore."

My grandmother's comment made me tear up as I considered she was willing to give everything for me. We all felt helpless but it was clear that I had a family that was there with me no matter what.

Her reaction mirrored my own urgency for an immediate solution, however irrational. I understood that people with this disease have to grow up sixty years overnight. Kids lose their childhood because their minds are occupied with worries about the future, while families stand by feeling helpless.

I stared at the disability placard on my desk and thought, "If my life is going to be shorter, and if I'm going to become progressively worse, then it's time to do something about it."

Searching the Internet one evening, I was primed for a "call-to-action." I found an article about a guy who had multiple sclerosis and who planned to ride his "trike" around the United States to raise awareness. He was featured in a photo, standing next to a low-profile machine with three wheels and lots of gears.

It looked fast.

I didn't know anything about recumbent trikes, but when I saw that photo, something shifted. *I could do that.*

The following week, I bought myself a trike.

I drove to Peregrine Bicycle Works in Chico, California, which specialized in recumbent trikes. The shop was in an industrial area, where the smell of roasting coffee wafted from a nearby operation. My senses tuned into the excitement of the moment.

Hugh, the owner, wheeled a recumbent trike into the parking lot and instructed me on the basics. Steering, pedaling, and braking all seemed pretty intuitive. As I put my feet on the pedals, I felt the power transfer from my feet to the rear wheel of the trike. I looked down and watched the ground pass beneath me.

I was stunned.

I could move this thing forward without a wobble. I could stop without falling over. I was able to travel under my own power. I maneuvered onto a road with no traffic and put more strength into each pedal stroke. I started going fast, maybe 16 or 18 mph, amazed at how I could propel myself forward, unaided. Up to this point, whenever I rode a bike my focus had been limited to a basic concern: *Please Kyle. Don't fall over.*

On the trike, I was glued to the ground, held down by gravity like a streamlined train.

"I can go anywhere on this thing," I thought.

We all live with limitations. We all struggle with a sense of deficit. Sometimes, we need to identify the features of the one thing that will propel us forward.

I found that thing.

I felt *possibility* riding around that parking lot. I couldn't grasp the big picture, but I sensed the arrival of a life-changing force, and it had three wheels.

My choice narrowed down to a Catrike Pocket (they did not make the 700 yet, which I now ride) and an ICE Qnt. I settled on the ICE, which had a longer wheelbase, and a steel frame with a stock weight of 42 pounds—pretty heavy. I thought the ICE would be better for long distance, more durable, and versatile. With three 20-inch wheels and 27 speeds, it was the kind of trike that could cross a country.

Besides, it was fire-red and matched my truck.

At the end of the day, I parked it in my living room, situated myself on the seat, leaned back, and closed my eyes.

Up to that point, disease had pushed me through each day accompanied by a nagging fear. I struggled to find words. My emotions crashed into objects, people, into hopes and desires. When you're twenty-two, you feel that intangible *want* driving you forward. I felt that *want* magnified tenfold by uncertainty. I had passed through my childhood, ignorant of my limited time on this earth, and now I faced a world where the ground disappeared beneath my feet.

It was time to make my own decisions.

As I looked out my living room window, I felt the potential of life, even if it was shaded by an unknown future. I reached back and touched the wheel of the trike, which sat just inches from the back of my head.

I knew in that moment, my life was about to change.

FREEDOM'S JUST ANOTHER WORD
FOR NOTHING LEFT TO LOSE

I may have been sidetracked by a college crush, but there wasn't a woman on the planet who could match the love affair with my red recumbent. My entire world hovered around her three wheels and her streamlined, high-tech steel chassis.

Sometimes, we must be obsessive about our desires. We must know what it feels like to exert 150 percent. When I started riding my trike, I couldn't sleep at night. I couldn't eat. My co-workers found me staring off into space, thinking about my next ride. I bought magazines. Searched the Internet for riding opportunities.

The trike offered me mobility, freedom, and independence. It offered me a chance to be an athlete again, and I wanted to capitalize on the momentum.

Whether I rode to a card game with friends, the market, or short trips through downtown Sacramento, I got on the trike every chance I got. I had little concept of safe or unsafe riding. I didn't have cycling shoes and clip-in pedals yet, and my steering was erratic. People yelled at me from their cars, the sidewalks, and street corners. Instead of navigating the city in my car, I began to experience my physical presence in a world dominated by machinery. I grew addicted to a simple fact: I could travel from my neighborhood under my own steam, and *get somewhere.*

Within weeks, I attempted my first fourteen-mile ride.

I had been living with friends Bryan and Cole at Third and P streets in Sacramento. The American River Parkway Bike Trail offered an entry point right across the street from our apartment. The paved trail followed the river on a raised levee, which offered views of the winding water, green-leafed canopies, endless rice fields, and distant foothills.

After I pushed off, I leaned back in my lounge chair, maintaining my speed at 10 mph. The trike was easy to steer, but also sensitive. With increased speed, I knew the trike could flip, so I didn't make any quick moves. Although I was eager to complete the distance, I kicked back and enjoyed the ride.

I felt total freedom, a sensation that seemed almost foreign. All of a sudden, I wasn't so different from anyone else. I was a guy going out for a bike ride, enjoying the river scenery, the clouds overhead, and the birds nesting along the shore.

But a few anxious thoughts filtered in. *What if I couldn't do it? What if I rode five miles and came to a grinding halt?* But I figured if I could make it to the end of the block, I could make it to another, and another.

As the days and weeks progressed, I challenged myself to go farther. Thirty miles. Sixty miles. I read about cycling culture. Talked to other cyclists. I began thinking, dreaming, consumed by this new force. For the first time in a while, I felt hope. It appeared on the periphery of my senses, challenging the black hole that had consumed my life.

Before my diagnosis, "hope" had been a warm and fuzzy concept, not one that defied the nature of my existence. As a boy, I could "hope" for a Christmas toy or an electronic gadget. However, with "disease" defining the conditions of my life, I grew cynical about the idea of hope. *How could hope exist alongside a progressive disease?*

During a forty-mile ride to Folsom from my apartment in Sacramento, I had hours to consider this question. About twenty miles into the ride, the answer seemed obvious: I had to act and make hope happen. So, I wondered, *exactly how far could I go?*

Across the United States, of course.

Soon after, I went to the 49th annual National Ataxia Foundation (NAF) Annual Membership Meeting in Boston. These conferences offer patients and families workshops to learn about current research, how to cope with ataxia, medical care, and insurance, but most importantly, they provide the opportunity to connect with other families.

I wanted to test the idea of my ride, but I was nervous. The entire concept felt self-indulgent. Here we are just trying to survive this disease, and I want to ride across the country.

At one of the dinners, I shared a table with several families. I passed around a photo of my recumbent like I was sharing a picture of my favorite pet (yeah, I was the kind of guy who carried a photo of my trike in my wallet).

"I'd like to ride 2,500 miles across the country on it," I told them—then nervously waited to see their expressions.

Mark Bogucki, who had traveled from Kansas, sat there with his family. His daughter, Lauren, was diagnosed with FA in her teens. The Bogucki family had been involved in the FA community for many years, and he was a man who wanted to make hope happen. He leaned forward with a serious expression.

"Okay," he said. "I'll give you one dollar per mile."

Then Norm Simpson, who has a son living with FA, chimed in.

"I'll throw in another $500 if you get it done," he said.

I was stunned. Until that moment, I couldn't predict if anyone would get behind my idea. I wasn't prepared for their quick support: Zero to $3,000 in ninety seconds.

But this meant I really had to do it. Now I had to figure out if my legs could carry me that far.

MY FIRST CENTURY RIDE:
A MILESTONE FOR EVERY CYCLIST

Most cyclists remember their first century—a hundred miles through varied terrain, where riders show up to challenge themselves rather than compete against one another. While most riders simply seek the thrill of watching their odometer click into triple digits for the first time, many fail because of poor training, dehydration, and overexertion.

I had learned about the century ride through my job at Brown and Caldwell, which had organized a team to raise money for the American Diabetes Association. I had a friend with diabetes, so I felt good about raising the required minimum $300, my first real experience with fundraising. A donation from my parents and a couple friends did the trick.

I had about a month to train and everything to lose. I was not an athlete. I had no idea how to train so I just rode a lot and I rode hard. I rode until my legs ached. I rode until my lungs burned.

When the weekend of the century ride arrived, I packed my trike into the back of my truck and drove to stay with a friend, Lindsey, who lived close to the ride route in Napa Valley.

I woke up at 4:30 AM in the spare room of Lindsey's place in Petaluma, one of those small Northern California towns where wealth and rural America meet. The entire region north of San Francisco coexists in a culture of coffee shops, mom-and-pop stores, cows dotting the hills, and Mercedes competing for road space with local tractors.

I smelled the cool morning air through the open window. Even in the darkness of the quiet room, I recognized the intensity of the day in front of me. I pulled on my long black tights and added a purple and gray cycling jersey with the Brown and Caldwell logo across the chest. That day I would be part of Team BC with other riders I would see on the route. I crept out and closed the door quietly behind me, but with my heart pounding and an anxious pit in my stomach, I could barely contain my excitement.

I was there to participate in the American Diabetes Association's Tour de Cure campaign. The course began and ended at Yountville, circling through idyllic, rolling hills in the heart of Wine Country.

My purpose was both in-service and functional. I was participating in an event to raise awareness about an illness, but my true purpose was clear: I wanted to prove to myself that I was an athlete. If I couldn't make this ride, how could I ride across the United States? If I failed, my dream was dead.

I arrived at the 6 AM registration, where hundreds of other riders had converged at the starting line.

Full water bottles. Check.

A few energy bars. Check.

Flag. Spare tubes. Pump. Check.

Riders were chatting and laughing, all clad in Lycra, their cycling cleats clicking on the pavement as they stood in line to turn in their last-minute donations.

It seemed like everyone knew each other. I was the outsider, the least experienced rider in the group, the guy who had logged only four months of cycling, the guy with the staggering gait, the guy who had the wide-eyed look of being out of his league.

I stumbled through the line, turned in my registration, got on the trike, and choked down a banana.

As I pulled on my gloves, my eyes scanned the edges of Napa Valley. Low fog hovered over lush green meadows. Oak trees dotted the landscape, where weathered fence posts and barn roofs intersected with million-dollar wineries. Rows of vineyards blanketed the hills, snaking into shallow gullies, then emerged again farther on, where a Victorian mansion would peer through the trees.

After the kickoff, I rode the first twelve miles shoulder-to-shoulder with the pack, wheels inches from each other at 20 mph, rolling down hills *en masse* and around sharp bends. One tap of the brake or lapse in concentration could send the whole bunch to the ground.

This was my first experience in a big group of riders, and I strained to keep pace. Although I knew this was a fundraiser, I felt the rush of competition. Other riders seemed pretty serious. When I got passed on the left, I would pedal harder. When a rider came up behind me, I would accelerate. I would pay for this waste of energy later, but I pushed on like this for fifty-five miles.

Then I got a flat.

"No problem," I thought, "I've got a spare tube." I pulled out the spare and discovered I had the wrong size. I felt my century ride slipping away.

In big charity rides, vehicles from local bike shops rove the course and provide mechanical support for the riders. After about twenty minutes waiting beside the road, the SAG truck pulled up to where I was parked next to a panel of rural mailboxes. The driver had a bunch of tubes but none of them fit, so we simply had to patch the tire.

By this time, all the riders were ahead of me. I was the only rider left. I sat on the tailgate, and waited for the glue to dry.

I had reached a rural part of the valley, where the distances between farms had increased. Even though the open landscape calmed my anxiety, I was thinking if I failed to make this ride, it would stop my forward momentum. Maybe it would prove that I really wasn't a cyclist.

Once I got back on the road, the rest stops were empty and packing up for the day. I was hungry and thirsty, but no one seemed to care. The day was over. *Hey!* I wanted to shout. *This is my big day. What's the deal here? Where are you going?*

A volunteer couple reluctantly pulled water jugs from their van so I could fill my bottles, and scrape the last bits of trail mix.

I pushed on, considerably slower. My water bottles went empty, the sun had dropped behind a mountain, and I was down to my last chocolate energy bar, which had melted from the heat.

I stopped on the empty road, wind hissing across the tall grass. A few birds darted from tree to tree. I contemplated the liquid chocolate in my hand and shrugged. Then I shoved the entire melted bar into my mouth, chocolate covering my face, my beard, and my fingers.

I licked my fingers and continued on. When I made it to the finish line, the tables and tents were all packed up, the banners removed. The riders had finished their rides, packed up their bikes, and gone home.

I heard a few cheers from the remaining volunteers, but none of them expressed the total satisfaction that I felt. I had made it, 100 miles in ten hours.

Now it was time for the next step.

YOU WANT TO RIDE WHERE?

My mother sees herself as a reasonable person. She might be disorganized, but on game day, without question, she's the one you want on your team.

Diane Bryant grew up in a single-story home in Oroville, California, wearing the clothes her mother made for her. Her father, Arthur Lacativo, worked as a business agent for the Oroville Dam Laborers Union during the dam construction in the early 1960s. The family never had much money, and, as a result, my mother grew up a resourceful and opinionated person. She never hesitated to wrestle my brother and I around to her point of view.

Whenever my brother got in the car with cigarette smoke on his breath, she would sing at the top of her lungs, "Smoker, smoker, you're gonna DIIEEE," like she was auditioning for the Grand Ole Opry. She wanted her boys to have steady jobs and big paychecks, not premature lung disease.

When I got a job as a project engineer on water and wastewater projects, she proudly referred to me as her "shitty engineer." I had done all the things I was supposed to do. I got good grades, went to college, got a respectable job. I had fulfilled her vision.

Now, with limited mobility and a progressive disease, riding a tricycle across the United States was *not* in her vision. It was not reasonable.

THIS CALLED FOR DINNER AT
OUTBACK STEAKHOUSE

We arrived at the restaurant before the dinner rush. My mother walked ahead, while I stumbled to the table. I ordered the chicken and shrimp pasta. She ordered the prime rib.

We sat in comfortable silence and buttered our bread. When we began to eat, I started my pitch.

"I've been going on long rides lately," I said.

"Yes, that ride in Napa was 100 miles?"

"Yep, I've been researching people who ride trikes across the country."

She moved her eyes from the plate, but kept her head down, still chewing.

"I think I could do that," I said, "ride across the country, that is."

She stopped chewing. Her shoulders sank, but her brow remained raised. I kept talking.

"You know ... to raise awareness and money for ataxia research." I tried to sound unselfish *for the ataxia community*, which was true, in part, but at this point my decision was about me.

Silence. More chewing. She looked down at her plate and shuffled potatoes with her fork. Around us, diners continued their animated conversations about the quality of the food, or baseball, or grades, or local politics.

"You remember how Mark Bogucki and Norm Simpson offered to fund a cross-country ride?" I said.

"Yes, I didn't think you were serious."

"I could ride to next year's NAF meeting in Memphis," I said, starting to blab. "It would be a 2,500-mile ride. I could visit Graceland. I would ride 50 miles a day. Cole said he might be interested and we could sleep in the bed of my truck. My goal is to raise $30,000..."

More silence. She thought I was nuts. This diagnosis had gone to my head. Why couldn't I just be happy with my (all things considered) fortunate situation? Why didn't I grasp how much additional stress this might place upon my family?

When we suffer, we forget the burden our loved ones carry. We leave little room to consider that our chaotic lives now share the same geography as our parents, our siblings, and those we love.

I considered this when my mother raised her head, looked me in the eye, and said, "I have one stipulation...I'm coming with you."

After dinner, my mom went home and pitched the idea to my dad. "Well, he thinks he's going to ride across the country six months *from now*."

"Okay," my dad said. End of conversation. He didn't seem interested.

My dad is a born-in-Montana man, a raised-in-Oroville-California-man, a hunting and fishing kind of man, a thirty-year insurance man whose father was an insurance man—a man who spent his career managing risks, not taking them.

So a bike ride across the United States? Forget it.

I imagine there were times in my dad's life when he wanted to reach beyond his grasp, but he held himself back out of obligation. He built a career, raised a family, did the right thing. Then when I was diagnosed, his world collapsed. In the mornings, he would sit with his newspaper and coffee at the table. The words blurred on the page as he thought about all the hopes and dreams for my life, crushed. He felt helpless. With his characteristic stoicism he would manage to utter, "Have a good day at school, Bud."

My disease had erased risk management. It erased neat and tidy. Our lives had changed, and he could no longer depend upon the known world. Perhaps if he ignored my mom's announcement, the reality might disappear.

But it didn't.

My mom waited a few weeks and told him again. "Well, he's still talking about riding across the country."

My dad, not a big talker, said, *"Okay."*

My mom mentioned the idea several more times over the course of several months, but he refused to register the information. She kept trying. "I don't think it's a good idea for him to go alone," she said. Finally, she threw down the gauntlet.

"Where do you think he's going to sleep…in a cornfield?" she asked, flustered.

So, my dad went out and bought himself a bike.

CHAPTER 2

When Infinity Knocked on My Door

Following a diagnosis of a life-threatening disease, you're metaphorically quarantined from the general population.

When that moment arrives, isolation is *not* your friend. It's not a cozy moment with a cup of tea in a Tibetan monastery, nor the view of a golden Patagonian sunset.

Instead, you've plunged off a cliff. Your limbs and body are in free fall over an unspecified ground. Trees, plants, buildings, and people barely take shape above the clouds. You might see a field or a city street filled with large trucks, but nothing more.

You'll hit the ground at some point, but with a progressive disease, that's an unspecified point.

It's more surreal than that. When you approach the finite, everything in your life circumscribes to that endpoint, and nothing looks familiar. The rules of convention shift. You see things through another lens.

When I meet another person with FA, few words can express what we already know. It's that shared recognition. *Oh, you're from my planet. You know the shape of my life.*

You understand how it feels to walk and lose control in front of a crowd, to experience that invisible force, the weight of that sudden "push" where you stumble and drop to the ground. You understand what it means to lose a basic function, which accompanies the progressive de-evolution of your healthy body as your physical acuity keeps moving backward.

More important, you recognize the isolation that accompanies each day.

It's hard to let people into that part of my life—the scary moments, the awkward thoughts, the disabling emotional fears. That's the forbidden part of my imagination, where I spend time with catastrophe. My life is sometimes overshadowed by the unsolvable problem.

I didn't experience this feeling right away. It crept up at awkward moments. I'd be standing in a market, contemplating a box of cereal, and the reality would hit me like a punch to the gut.

Not long after my diagnosis, I read an article by Michelle Willems, who had lost her father to spinocerebellar ataxia—a disease that shares the same degenerative properties as Friedreich's ataxia. She describes watching the progression of her father's disease. At that time, a solid diagnosis for his type of disease was rare. As the years progressed, she watched her father stagger from room to room, each year marking a greater physical loss, until the walls, door jambs, and counters of their home bore indelible scars from his clutching fingers.

I sat in my parents' living room with the red couches and the brown carpet and the La-Z-Boy and my mom's burning candles. Family photos cluttered the shelves—the four of us at the top of Haleakala; me doing a 360 on my kneeboard; my parents' wedding. I looked up from the couch and checked the door jambs. I could see faint handprints appearing on the walls and door jambs in each room.

I turned my attention back to the article. The woman describes how, in her father's terminal stage, he struggled with dysphagia —paralysis of the throat muscles—a condition that cut off his communication, silenced the man forever, and signaled a system collapse, which eventually ended in heart failure.

That's when it hit me.

I'd been choosing to ignore my future. Until that moment, I didn't want to talk about, look at, think about, or honestly face this disease. I wanted to stow it away, and forget about it. I wanted to compartmentalize the narrative.

In that moment I thought, *I'll never be as able-bodied as I am right now.* I had no idea what was going to happen. I couldn't predict the progression of FA in the next six months or in the next ten years. My life had assumed an uncertainty that placed me on permanent fight or flight.

I had to figure out how to take back control.

A GOLF TOURNAMENT TURNS
INTO $10,000

With the notion of my ride accelerating, my hometown of Lake of the Pines, California, got wind of the idea and organized a golf tournament to raise money.

The response from our friends, neighbors, and family was overwhelming. My uncle flew in from Montana, my brother and his friends came down from Chico, other friends arrived from around the state. The tournament took place at the Lake of the Pines Golf Club, less than a mile from our house. We ended up with twenty-four teams of four and twenty-eight hole sponsors. When the tournament ended, organizer Harry Lent handed me a check for $9,800. While the ride was designed to raise money for research, we needed this cash gift to underwrite trip expenses.

As the weeks rolled toward our departure date, we were blown away by every donation for research. A check would arrive for $25 from someone we hadn't heard from in five years, and we would cheer. We were able to reconnect with friends from a place of pride rather than shame because we were doing something about our situation. Rather than *please help me because I have this horrible disease*, the cross-country ride offered an alternative dialogue: *Okay. We were dealt this unfortunate hand. Here is what we're doing about it. Would you like to take part?*

Ultimately, when people contribute to a fundraising effort, it's not about the money. Sure, when someone hands you money, it's pretty cool, but the reward arrives when you see how people value you and what you're doing.

The days of aggressive Internet campaigns had yet to manifest, where you launch a web page, and appeal to the sympathies of supporters. Instead, people made phone calls. Networked. Had conversations. Showed up. Physical bodies moving toward a tangible goal. It worked.

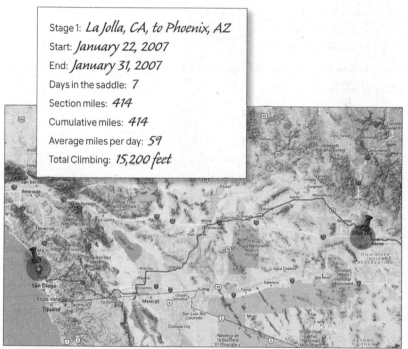

Stage 1: *La Jolla, CA, to Phoenix, AZ*
Start: *January 22, 2007*
End: *January 31, 2007*
Days in the saddle: *7*
Section miles: *414*
Cumulative miles: *414*
Average miles per day: *59*
Total Climbing: *15,200 feet*

Map data ©2018 Google via ridewithgps.com.

WITH MY BACK AGAINST A
CALIFORNIA COASTLINE

I was already sweating, probably from anxiety. I steered my trike through the shadows of the early morning sun, watching the horizon beyond the rooflines and the buildings, beyond the highways and the tract homes that bisected the coastal community of La Jolla, California. I noted the deep blue sky that marked the distance, where brown coastal foothills rose to the east. The pungent ocean stirred behind me, where seals lounged on the rocks.

I checked the mirror mounted on my left handlebar, and watched the size of the crowd diminish—the balloons, the cheering, the local television networks, my friends and family, all who had assembled for the send-off from the Scripps Research Institute parking lot.

The lab of Dr. Joel Gottesfeld had recently made a promising discovery in FA research at Scripps and we were glad to help draw a little attention to his work.

My mirror framed several banners, which snapped in the ocean breeze a few blocks behind me. Two ataxia organizations had arrived to support my ride—the National Ataxia Foundation (NAF), and the Friedreich's Ataxia Research Alliance (FARA). *That* was significant.

While both organizations are ultimately aligned to serve their patient communities, there is a clear difference in their missions: NAF, founded in 1957, is dedicated to patient advocacy and support for all types of ataxia-related diseases. And FARA, founded in 1998, raises money for research that specifically targets Friedreich's ataxia.

Differences in mission can be a sticking point when collaborating in nonprofits, where altruism and pragmatism frequently collide. Decisions must be made about how and where resources should be allocated.

Ron Bartek, the president of FARA, had flown out from Virginia. I hardly knew Ron at the time, but I felt tremendous respect for the man. He made a strong show for my send-off. This was a big deal.

A graduate of the U.S. Military Academy at West Point, Ron served four years in the Army, including as a company commander in Korea and a military intelligence officer in Vietnam. His career trajectory brought him to the State Department, where he worked in defense and foreign policy, including as a negotiator on the U.S. delegation to the Intermediate-Range Nuclear Forces Treaty in Geneva. Ron lived one of his dreams when he helped deliver the Treaty for signature by Presidents Reagan and Gorbachev.

While his life had such noble and heroic aspects, I was keenly interested in Ron's current mission: Finding a cure for Friedreich's ataxia.

When Ron founded FARA with his wife Raychel in 1998, their son Keith had been diagnosed with Friedreich's ataxia a year earlier. The couple had entered the familiar vacuum, where families struggled alone with limited facts of the disease and virtually no community. The FA gene had been identified a year earlier, but little information reached the patient community. Ron and Raychel understood how governing bodies accelerate research and the spread of information, so they created FARA, instilling the spirit of collaboration into the core of the organization.

During the months leading up to my ride, Ron had communicated with Mike Parent, executive director at NAF. Both knew their organizations were significant to me. The first time I had met someone with FA was at a NAF conference, and FARA's strong focus on FA while maintaining a culture of collaboration resonated with me.

Both organizations—including NAF's San Diego chapter president Earl McLaughlin—came to the California starting line to support my ride.

Sandy Lane, one of FARA's founding board directors, came from Orange County for the event, too. In honor of her daughter Chelsea, she had been involved in some of the first large-scale fundraisers for FARA, walks that raised several hundred thousand dollars. I was honored to have them all there.

I wore my newly printed *rideATAXIA* jersey, sunglasses, and my helmet as I prepared to depart. Chelsea could not maneuver her wheelchair and she had a hard time speaking so I leaned in close as Sandy pushed her up to me. Even with FA taking control of her body, Chelsea mustered a show of character when she said, "Work it!"

After the final round of photos, I stood in the parking lot next to my trike. The sun peeked over the mountains to the east. I tasted salt on my lips, which blew in from waves churning off the bluffs.

rideATAXIA was a fundraising ride, and I wanted to donate the proceeds in a productive direction, but I couldn't figure out where to commit the funds.

Ron saw that I had grown silent, and he walked up to me. "NAF and FARA have both been important to my family," I said. "And I'm going to have to make a decision about the funding from this ride."

Ron placed his hands on my shoulders and nodded at my trike. Then he looked me in the eye.

"Kyle," he said, "that trike right there is going to be a vehicle of change."

For a moment the chaos dimmed.

His comment mirrored the larger-than-life journey that had begun six months earlier when I committed to the ride. On the outside, I conveyed the picture of grins and smiles and hand-shakes. On the inside, I felt the weight of the entire FA community on my shoulders.

Though the idea had not taken shape yet, this was the beginning of a collaborative relationship between FARA and NAF and perhaps a model for future collaborations. Ron proposed that we split the proceeds between FARA and NAF, hoping that the two organizations would create a matching grant together. The organizations would examine the idea further, while I journeyed across the United States.

I thought about the hundreds of families in the extended FA community rallying around a singular concept—permission to feel hope. With a debilitating disease, your life expectations grow thin. The concept of a future feels foreign—even uncomfortable—a by-product of the shopping list of dismal symptoms that accompany the disease. But when a collective gathers with a singular focus, you're allowed to glimpse outside the boundaries.

I had stepped into the FA community without much planning, and now I had become an agent of change, or at least my trike had, which took some of the pressure off. When Ron made his proclamation, he wasn't throwing around fuzzy abstractions. Change had already begun. People were thinking: If we raise *real* momentum for research *and* create national awareness, maybe we can kick this thing. Maybe we can find a cure.

Three minutes later, I rode out of the parking lot.

Seven other cyclists pedaled with me, friends of the family who joined us for a symbolic start. They included John Hartigan and Paul Monson, who remained with our team for several days.

John's daughter Ashley was diagnosed with FA and their family lived in a suburb of Sacramento. John was a monster cyclist who had completed multiple double centuries (200 miles in a day) and he and Paul were part of a group that participated in RAGBRAI (a huge ride across Iowa) each year.

We were happy to have their depth of experience and drive to get us going on the first few days.

Within twenty miles, the remaining team would include John and Paul, my dad, my mom (at the wheel of our shiny new Dodge Durango, travel trailer in tow), and me.

But for the moment, we were a cluster of cyclists, working as a single unit. We crossed drainage canals, short stretches of bike trails, and rural highways, trying to shake off the city streets. We wanted to hit the frontier, that transition point where civilization fell away. We called out to each other, deciding upon which roads to take, gearing up for the gradual increase in elevation. Everybody was juiced.

Just getting out of San Diego proper took most of the day, negotiating traffic, highways, and red lights, strip malls, and freeway overpasses. But the coastal foothills lured us ahead to the ascent that would take us to the southern deserts and beyond.

In my gear bag in the support vehicle, along with my jerseys, shorts, long-sleeve shirts, gloves, jackets, and tights, I had a leather pouch that a mother—Heidi Mazeres, whose son has FA—sent me before the trip. It contained a smashed penny, an amethyst, and a turquoise stone with a hemp string tied around it. They were meant to bring good luck.

A note had accompanied Heidi's package: *"You have the courage to take a stand. May you be blessed beyond measure all the days of your life."*

That was the kind of sentiment that spurred me forward, a message that confirmed my quest and pumped me with pride as I left the starting line behind. With narratives like this, I could have easily embraced the messianic scale of the trip. Fortunately, there's always someone to temper our heroic journeys.

Heidi's note contrasted with a different message that someone sent me on Facebook: "*I bet you love having FA. Makes you feel special. We're fucked. Stop your crusade, poster boy. Why don't you show people the real FA? Like someone wiping your ass or feeding you dinner? Riding your little bike does nothing.*"

This guy knew how to cut deep, and it pissed me off, but he was partly right.

His statement affirmed what I had been feeling. I was in pretty great shape. What could I complain about? There are many devastating symptoms of FA, but at that time I only experienced a few. I had early symptoms of scoliosis, and mild balance and coordination issues, and that was it. I wasn't eating out of a tube. I wasn't dealing with heart complications. I could still use the toilet on my own.

The real physical trauma happens to children in advanced stages of the disease.

As FA progresses, some children can't speak because their diaphragm and the muscles in their mouth are compromised. Many struggle to breathe. Eating food turns into a near death experience because of the difficulty swallowing. Many young adults require a catheter to go to the bathroom, which can promote infections that can become life-threatening. A simple cold can turn into a pneumonia that doctors can't control.

Every day, families anticipate a cardiac event, when their child falls to the ground on the living room floor, complaining of chest pains.

I wanted everything to be rosy and bright, but I wasn't going to escape this reality. This was my future, and maybe a bike ride *wasn't* going to fix it. Maybe the entire adventure created false hope.

I felt the weight of many individuals and families who suffered more intensely. Perhaps I was still in denial, hoping to circumvent reality. Perhaps I *was* trying to be a poster boy. I was young and naive, and I still felt invincible. These two conflicts—my urgency to *do* something, and my survivor's guilt—were tearing me apart.

Fortunately, I felt a larger framework creeping in—the presence of a growing community coalescing behind an idea, which defined itself by a feature even more profound than the disease: hope.

I felt this strength in numbers. People weren't supporting the ride because I was a hero, but because "community" offered a path out of the isolation and despair.

With all of this swirling in my head, I focused on my ascent into the foothills.

WHEN RIDING ACROSS A RING OF FIRE, WEAR PROPER SHOES

After our entourage departed and returned to their jobs and families and lives, my dad and I rode deeper into the Laguna Mountains, a stretch of steep canyons and valleys attached to the Peninsular Range—a thousand miles of scrub oak, pine, and trickling creeks, extending from the eastern San Diego County foothills down through Baja California, where a carpet of country obscured the presence of scrawny coyotes, deer, bobcats, and mountain lions who roamed the canyons on the fringes of civilization.

We rode across an ancient seabed, which rose above the same granite rock that supported the entire Sierra Nevada mountain range, created about 120 million years ago—part of the "Ring of Fire," a geological phenomenon that rims 25,000 miles of the Pacific Ocean—452 volcanoes and shifting tectonic plates where 90 percent of the earth's earthquakes occur.

Geologic formations ensure a constant state of change, but dramatic change occurs—the upheavals and explosions, earthquakes and landmass shifts—when resistance gives way to the inevitability of transformation.

We often believe we have the luxury of choice, but our lives are weighed down by inertia, our days defined by resistance to change. It's a miracle anything ever occurs, but when it does, the force can be sudden and unexpected, even violent.

I may have pedaled forward out of necessity, out of the need to act, and I may have convinced myself that this decision grew out of choice, but my circumstances were beyond my control, and I'm not referring to the reaction to my disease. I'm referring to the conditions of my life as it unfolded *as a result of the disease.*

When serious discord overshadows our lives, and threatens to dismantle the world as we know it, we only have one choice—to push back. This is where choice *does* influence our actions, how we choose to push, the quality of our lean, from the smallest daily decisions to the largest.

What's the alternative? If we surrender entirely to our fate, then we lose the opportunities to affect the small steps in-between.

But my "push" wasn't the work of a single individual deter-mined to overcome adversity. The outcome of my actions drew upon the contributions of many individuals, filling the void behind me, leaning into that adversity—my mom getting on board, community fundraising, and families sending small dona-tions. When we surrender the need to control our circumstances, where nobody's more important than anyone else, then each indi-vidual fulfills his or her unique role toward the outcome.

Once I started to understand my role in the larger framework, I could focus on my immediate conditions. I was able to assess my reactions in "real-time," and objectively evaluate how to respond. As soon as I left my cubicle, I was able to slow down and make decisions that mattered.

For example, during long ride intervals, if I anticipated the vast miles ahead, I might have surrendered any notion of succeeding, and decided to take the next bus to Memphis. Traversing the distance of a continent does, indeed, mess with your mind. The impossibility maintains constant pressure.

Take the simple mapping of our journey. The actual planning felt overwhelming. With today's technology, any cross-country ride would take five minutes to search the route online, download the details to your phone and off you go. But in 2007, mapping our actual route was a nightmare.

After I ordered maps online from the Adventure Cycling Asso-ciation in Billings, Montana, they sent me seven physical maps of the route, broken down into sections. I had selected the maps for the Southern Tier, and spent days pouring over the geographic segments and locations of RV campgrounds, which were spaced fifty miles apart to meet our daily ride intervals.

Now, picture my dad and me standing out in the middle of the Arizona desert in a blasting wind, trying to make sense of an enormous map. The most technologically advanced thing about those maps? They were waterproof.

It was easy to feel crushed as we looked ahead. But I knew that being overwhelmed or consumed with thoughts of failure would impact hundreds, if not thousands, of people. While that thought terrified me, I could no longer satisfy my own insecurities.

As a solution, I focused on the revolution of the cranks, over and over, the hypnotic rising and falling, the road passing beneath, the rhythmic glint of the steel cranks, the teeth grabbing and releasing the chain as I moved forward. The gaze helped me focus on my breathing, which drove the sheer physical effort. Occasionally, I glanced at the horizon, where the mountains and the clouds encountered blue sky, punctuated by circling birds, or an airplane miles above.

Within this bubble of "presence," I felt more alive than ever.

So we aimed up the mountain, which demanded an elevation rise from a few hundred feet to 4,000, eventually dropping us down into the Anza-Borrego Desert where we would power across the Southwest.

That's where the problems started.

Almost immediately after our departure, my iliotibial band (IT band) started to burn. The IT band is a connective tissue—vital to knee stabilization—that plays a crucial role in bending your knee. IT band injuries are common for runners (and for novice cyclists).

The explanation was simple: When I blasted from Sacramento to San Francisco a few months earlier, with the intent to train myself into readiness for this trip, I inflamed that region on my left knee. About sixty miles into that ride, the tendon tightened, complained, and screamed, *Slow down!*

But I pushed ahead out of urgency. I had virtually no training. My experience had been limited to the century ride and trail rides along the Sacramento River, so I pushed hard without any intelligent design in my training.

After the San Francisco ride, I returned home, visited the doctor, got a cortisone shot—really a Band-Aid to mask the pain —packed my gear, took a leave of absence from my job, drove to San Diego, and got on my trike for a cross-country trip. I was skilled at ignoring pain, after years of stitches and broken bones, and I was determined to ignore this one.

As my dad and I ascended the mountain, I tuned in to the smell of sweet black sage, and canyon chaparral, damp from the morning air. I distracted myself with reverie, watching the crisp January sky, a few hawks circling overhead, and the wind blowing through the trees.

But it wasn't working. Some of it resulted from the limitations of my machine. On a recumbent, any ascent is all on the legs. At least with an upright bike, your center of gravity sits above the pedals, so you can shift your body weight over the pedals for propulsion. On a trike, your body weight is removed from the equation, and you depend upon the force from your quads, which places extra stress on your knees. Then you've got the added resistance from the third wheel, which translates to more rubber on the road.

More resistance. More push. More knee pain. How was I going to make it 2,450 more miles?

As I navigated these thoughts, I told my dad about my knee. He was quiet for a moment.

"Well, let's just work through it," he said, "because you're not going to need your knee in the future."

That's a typical thing my dad might say. He didn't know what other advice to offer. We both knew my knee wasn't going to improve, and it didn't matter anyway. In a few years, I wouldn't be walking. The comment may have seemed insensitive, but it was the opposite of thoughtless.

My dad and I never discussed my disease directly. We never knew what to say, and while he made light of the situation, we both knew what he meant. We were having a conversation without having one.

I respected him for stepping out of his comfort zone and taking a risk by acknowledging my predicament, and even downplaying the burden.

When I conceived a ride across the United States, with my physical abilities declining and an unknown end looming, it was an opportunity to face the unpredictability that had consumed our lives, but that unpredictability didn't include a 2,500-mile bike ride.

My dad couldn't conceive of completing more than a few hours on a bike, much less two months. A cross-country adventure wasn't on his bucket list.

When he started training three months before the trip, he rode six to eight miles a few times a week. People said, "Oh no, you have to train twenty miles a day. There's no way you guys can make it otherwise." Typically, my dad has to picture something to understand how to accomplish the task. He had no picture for this cross-country trip. It wasn't going to happen, so why prepare seriously?

Just before we hit the summit on Interstate 8 in Cleveland National Forest, I looked over at him, clipped into his brand-new bike, a Specialized Allez. He wore his official *rideATAXIA* jersey that had been delivered days earlier, along with his new helmet, sunglasses with rearview mirror attached, and Lycra bike shorts and shoes. While he worked the pedals, head down, shoulders hunched, sweat glistening from his forehead, his eyes scanned the sky above the Anza-Borrego Desert, which waited fifteen miles below, gateway to hundreds of miles through the Southwestern deserts, where wind and dust and stars marked the journey ahead.

When we dropped over the summit at 4,000 feet, we had a crazy downhill that would usher us all the way into the desert floor. As soon as we began our descent, my speedometer hit 30 mph, and I wasn't even pedaling.

It might be hard going up on a recumbent, but you can kick ass going down. Less wind resistance + low center of gravity = haul ass.

But speed arrives with challenges—like rumble strips. When you're on the open road, most interstate highways have a rumble-strip, a corrugated section that lets drivers know that they are drifting off the highway and into the unknown...and into anything (or anyone) who happens to be on the other side of that strip.

For cross-country cyclists, the rumble strip is always a big presence. When you hear a big truck drifting onto the rumble strip five seconds behind you, it's pretty clear that the end is near.

After the grueling ride up, speed was the essential antidote on the way down. We needed to shake loose the fight with gravity. Not long after the summit, the grade grew steeper, the shoulder grew smaller, and cars and trucks passed within feet. I grew cognizant of the narrowing choice between pitching into the canyon below, or getting flattened by a car.

The only option was to push my speed. Any downhill acceleration turns my single rear wheel into a rudder. A little lean to the left, and I'm sailing into the road. A little lean to the right and I'm over the edge of the cliff. If the rudder loses contact with the ground, control is gone. Every time the shoulder disappeared, I had to cross the rumble strip, and the added kick made my back wheel bounce around like a rubber ball.

Cactus, shrub, and black sage flew past, a mad speed pulling me down the road. I was losing control, but I didn't care.

The total rush, reckless speed, the wind in my face, and then the cars hitting the rumble strip at 70 mph—I could barely contain my excitement.

I was alive.

I gripped the handlebars and pushed on the pedals to gain more speed. I was pushing my body against the edge of the continent, where my life had merged with my wheels on the road. I was learning a new set of rules. I could talk about "facing my fears," but that's just talk. I could surrender to hopelessness, but that's hopelessness. Or I could learn how to raise my head and see what's next.

Across the desert, I scanned the Mexican border; a line in the desert separating the two nations, in some places a towering wall, in others, a stretch of barbed wire that signified the ambiguity built into every relationship. I saw a thin layer of orange sky hovering over gray mountains, where dusty border towns lay beneath the southern sun.

In a few short years, my identity had changed from high school athlete and prom king to the young man with the progressive disability, soon to be in a wheelchair. We can't know ourselves until we're willing to confront our insecurities. My disease had brought me into the presence of a life where I was forced to wake up.

I finally found my rhythm down the outer edge of a long sweeping curve. I steadied my breathing and I got my trike under control. When I calmed down, my rig responded and we coasted for another eight miles, until we reached flat ground.

After we hit the desert, I tasted grit and dust and low humidity that would suck the skin off your face. We pedaled into an expanse that stretched for hundreds of miles, where a different America emerged, an America that contrasted with my limited experience as a small-town Northern California boy. My America had pine trees and lush valleys where creeks ran lazy with fish, and furry wildlife padded through the undergrowth.

This America boasted sand dunes and cactus, where RVs and ATVs ran wild, and the wildlife was hard-shelled with scales and spikes and too many teeth. As we rode for hours beneath the dusty sun, signs of civil society disappeared. We traced the edge of a nation, where people flock to live on their own terms and step away from the conventions of social niceties.

When we reached giant sand dunes east of El Centro, the highway shoulder was diminished to a four-inch strip. We were forced to skim along the sand, which butted up against the highway. In the distance, motorcycles, dune buggies, and ATVs hugged the contours in every direction. It was Friday afternoon and all the weekend warriors were headed to the desert fueled by beer and Jack Daniels in their oversized RVs with motorized toys in tow. At one point, my dad, in an attempt to make room for one of the behemoth RVs bearing down on us, rode into the sand and fell over.

Soon we hit a stretch of road where the shoulder disappeared completely, and our line of sight vanished because of the hilly terrain. With the loss of buffer between our bikes and the fast-moving cars—in addition to minimal visibility—the situation grew sketchy. We pulled over into the dirt to discuss our options.

"Let's get in the car," my dad said.

I didn't want this to be an option. It meant a symbolic failure. A cross-country ride meant just that—tires on the road committing to every inch. Obstacles were inevitable, but I didn't want to jump in the car every few days. On the other hand, I knew this ride meant taking control of our lives, not losing them. On that stretch of road, death seemed like a possibility.

I relented to common sense. We loaded our gear into the truck. As we drove to a safer stretch of road, my stomach twisted into knots. My fingers clenched. I couldn't breathe.

"No one can know about this," I blurted. "I want to do what I said. We're not here to get in the car."

I was aware how petulant and impatient I sounded, but I had to say something. We just trashed the entire concept of the ride. I stared out the window. Along the edge of the highway, a few tumbleweeds blew across the dirt as we passed beneath the shadow of a mountain.

"Nobody's going to fault you, Kyle," my mom said.

I threw back a worn-out reaction that I had adopted when I faced any hardship: "It's not *supposed* to be easy," I shot back.

My mom rolled her eyes. "I hate it when you say that."

Lately, I'd been beating that statement to death. I was determined to outpace my disease, and that meant being okay with living hard. I thought about the woman whose father had left black marks throughout the house, his fingerprints a testament to his relentlessness. I wanted to honor that man, and complete what I set out to do.

When I first read that article, I was at a miserable stage of denial. I didn't want anything to do with Friedreich's ataxia. I didn't want anyone to know, and I tried my best to hide it. After I read the article, I sat on the couch staring at the walls. I was thinking about breathing tubes and wheelchairs and years of dependency when my parents walked in.

"This isn't the worst thing that has ever happened to anyone," I said. But we all knew the real subtext: *This is the worst thing that has ever happened to anyone.*

My dad sank into one of the chairs, then leaned forward and responded after a characteristic silence.

"Well. It's happening to you. It's happening to us. So, let's deal with it."

Somehow, we had reached the end of our denial. We had to move *toward* the disease, not away from it.

That was the turning point. We were finally saying *It's a shitty situation. We didn't think it could happen to us. But it is.* Somehow, it gave us permission to get out from underneath our fear and move ahead.

NOT EVERYONE IN ARIZONA
WEARS PANTS

Twenty miles after we passed the Colorado River, we paused on a ridge above the town of Quartzite, 250 miles from our starting point. The terrain was scrubbed dry for miles—the sun's glare blurring the mountains to the east.

Before we rolled down the hill, I paused on my trike. A sea of white motorhomes stretched across the valley, where thousands of rectangular trailers, tents, cars, motorcycles, and travelers spread across the landscape.

In summer, Quartzite claims a small desert population of 3,000 people, but during the winter months—December through February—that swells up to a million, according to the Arizona Highway Department. This snowbird mecca attracts visitors for the annual "rock hound" festivities, where an open-air market sells handmade arts and crafts, with "shows" that specialize in precious gems and minerals and people arrive from all directions for the festivities.

The view confounded the surrounding desolation. Thousands of RVs formed a giant parking lot that extended toward the horizon, rows upon rows upon rows of white recreation vehicles. Large red-and-white tents housed the main gem and mineral shows in the center of the arrangement. Other vendors and makeshift tents lined the main street.

After a gentle two-mile downhill, we rode along Main Street. The atmosphere was a mixture of carnival and yard sale, flea market and open-air stalls. The air reeked of hot dogs and funnel cake. Dirt and sand blew in every direction. Elderly folks with fanny packs roamed the streets. Dogs barked, some tied to ropes and kicking up dust. And big trucks pulled out of side roads and roared away.

I pedaled slowly through the chaos and thought, *I just rode my bike here.* Perhaps seasoned long-distance cyclists lose that novelty, but the magnitude of my experience was sinking in.

Mom roared up in the truck. "You guys have got to see this."

We threw our bikes in the back and drove back down the road. We pulled into a dirt lot with a single-story shack at one end with corrugated roofing. A man stood in front, the proud owner of the "Reader's Oasis" bookstore. His skin was brown and shriveled from the constant heat and sun. He wore a cowboy hat, full beard, long gray hair, sunglasses, and a blue fleece sweatshirt.

Below his waist, he wore nothing.

His "package" was tucked into a crocheted pouch with a small abalone shell on the outside—his family jewels. The entire outfit was completed with a pair of brown moccasins. Then we walked into the store and encountered a life-size cardboard cutout of the same man. Other tourists passed through the store and stared at him sideways, giggling under their breath.

I walked up to Paul and shook his hand. He was talkative and interested in our adventure. He was proud of living off the grid. "I've been running this store for seventeen years," he said. He had been a nudist for longer than that.

At one point, mid-sentence, he ran into his store and we're thinking, *This guy is nuts!* He returned with a book about a family who had crossed the country on bike, *How Many Hills to Hillsboro*, and offered it as a gift for our journey. So here we are judging this guy by his clothes (or lack thereof), and he's thinking about how he can serve others. He wasn't on a soapbox promoting his nudist views. He just liked being nude.

If you ignore the physical details of our semi-naked cowboy, if you take no offense at his beliefs, then he's just a guy who owns a bookstore. I'm thinking if I'm going to survive this disease, I need to be that guy—well, not particularly a nudist bookstore owner—but a guy who lives on his own terms.

The atmosphere in Quartzite affirmed my purpose. Here was a town on the fringes of society, where people invented their lives. They weren't trying to fit in or struggle against marginalization. They were running the show. I wanted to live by a similar notion, and this offbeat community on the edge of the desert gave me permission.

This feeling diminished the power of infinity, which had continued to hover over me. I was no longer in free fall, where my disease relentlessly confirmed the finite. Instead, the ground, the buildings, and the trees had become recognizable features, not the fuzzy unknown that was so terrifying, but the outlines of a future that offered shape to unlimited possibilities.

After we said our goodbyes, we drove to the Cove RV Resort back over the border in California. We had a beer and some cheese and crackers, then spaghetti and meatballs as we lounged beside the Colorado River, which was reduced to a trickle at this point. We stared out across the dry desert as the sun dropped behind the mountains.

The next day, we rode deep into the Arizona desert (fully clothed).

CHAPTER 3

This Ride
for Ballers Only

The American desert offers man the opportunity to regard his world through a vast lens—especially a man pedaling with his butt low to the ground.

Instead of the typical road trip, punctuated by fast-food islands, greasy French fries, and the stifling interior of your automobile, when you're on a trike you become a three-wheeled speck, moving across the surface of the earth, across a desert plain, beneath an immense blue sky, where you keep company with tumbleweeds, dust, and speeding cars.

When you're staring at this endless space for hours, you'd think your mind might tilt toward bigger things.

You'd think you might consider the meaning of existence. You'd think an answer might come forth, revealing a deeper understanding of the eternal battle of man versus nature. After all, you're staring at infinity, a landscape defined by space and time.

But the answer doesn't come.

Instead, you watch the clouds shift to the south. You pass a collapsed homestead to the north. You scan the shadowed canyons of a distant mountain range. And you think, sure, contemplating existence is a grandiose thing, but in order to experience the sublime, you pedal toward what's in front of you.

In other words, infinity doesn't look like forever. It's much closer than you think.

After a continuous week of riding, grinding it out on the road and 2,000 miles to go, living in the moment took on greater meaning. When I was informed that my disease guaranteed a physical decline, motor function loss, and premature death, I felt immediately powerless.

The doctors handed us a brochure and said, "Sorry."

My reaction was complex—denial as well as relief. While we finally had an answer, I didn't want to accept the situation. I faced terminology about a rare disease that was beyond my reach and the reach of my family. Most people who receive the diagnosis of a genetic and incurable disease face a guaranteed devastation. They look to their doctors for answers and find none. They look to the research community and discover impenetrable medical jargon. They look to the world and realize their options have narrowed.

It's easy to feel hopeless.

My purpose behind this trip was to change that story for myself and perhaps others. Although it wasn't clear at the time,

I wanted to redefine how people with disease interface with the *understanding of disease.* While the medical community offers well-intentioned intervention, this doesn't help us live our lives more effectively. Instead, seeking knowledge is a necessary first step. When a rare (and relatively unknown) disease enters your life, you must learn how to manage the flow of information.

That's when knowledge can empower your entire community.

With the help of FARA and NAF, I arranged meetings with three research facilities in Arizona, Houston, and New Orleans, which would occur during the course of my ride across the United States.

I wanted to see behind the scenes to learn whether a "cure" was even a possibility.

As we approached the outskirts of Phoenix, a line of civilization appeared in the sand. I steered into the suburban sprawl and aimed my trike toward our first target: the Biodesign Institute at Arizona State University.

Phoenix proper is not just a city. It's a spreading flood, a horizontal landscape of endless tract houses, moving across the desert at an alarming rate. By land area, Phoenix is one of the largest cities in the United States, and one of the fastest growing.

How was I supposed to push through *that?*

We rode toward this desert metropolis under a pastel sky. We transitioned to high alert—heavy car presence, sprawling highways, traffic lights, and rules of the road. After a week on desert highways, a big city was daunting. Traffic became more frenetic, and the industrial buildings turned into houses, sprawling corporate centers, and strip malls.

We went into survival mode.

At one point, I had to stop quickly, and my dad crashed into the back of my trike because we were both focused on the traffic.

Thankfully, our map led us along a series of urban bike trails, skirting concrete canals, until we reached Tempe, our final destination, which situated us near ASU.

When the Biodesign Institute opened its doors in 2004, its mission was to build a transparent team of biologists, chemists, physicians, engineers, and computer scientists. The collaboration promised to explore some of the most challenging problems in human health.

FARA had provided the institute with a healthy research grant to support their investigation into identifying novel treatments that target the mitochondrial dysfunction of Friedreich's ataxia. The research team led by Dr. Sidney Hecht was focused on mitochondrial dysfunction, which is the shared link to many diseases, including Parkinson's, Alzheimer's, and Lou Gehrig's disease (ALS).

This places FA in a class of diseases that impacts millions through a dysfunction in the body's energy production processes. As a result, a team of scientists, researchers, and even a welcome banner greeted my arrival in the lobby of the new unit of the research facility called the Center for BioEnergetics.

After we rolled our bikes into the lobby, my eyes landed on seventeen-year-old Brandon, who sat in a wheelchair next to his mother, surrounded by a cluster of scientists and administrators. He wore a black sweatshirt, black jeans, and a black hat turned backwards. He sat very straight, no doubt forced upright by the pain radiating from the metal rod screwed into his back.

More than half of FA patients under twenty are forced to have spinal fusion surgery to correct aggressive scoliosis that's partly due to the progression of the disease while the body is still developing.

Brandon's FA manifested much earlier than mine. As a result, his symptoms had progressed more quickly. His spine had reached a point where it began to push into his diaphragm and impede his breathing. The disease was slowly suffocating him.

Spinal fusion is crazy, medieval-type-stuff—rods and screws holding your body together. More than half of children with neuromuscular diseases are inevitable candidates for corrective surgery.

This progression mirrors a certain reality. FA is a neurological disaster zone, like Parkinson's, ALS, and other similar diseases that impede a body's ability to organize itself the way it was meant to. As the disease twists the musculoskeletal system, the architecture of the body reacts unfavorably.

For many, spinal fusion surgery becomes inescapable.

I watched Brandon's half-opened eyes as they tracked me across the lobby. Bands of sunlight streamed through the floor-to-ceiling windows. His eyes settled on my red trike, now parked on the expansive floor of the new wing. I saw a glimmer of envy and then a flash of anger.

I lurched toward his wheelchair with an outstretched hand.

"Hey brother," I said. "Sorry about your surgery."

I tried to muster an enthusiastic, cheery sentiment, "We're all in this together," or something like that, but I felt like a complete idiot.

"Yeah" is all he said. Then a long silence.

He probably wanted to say something more honest like, "What the hell are you so happy about?"

Amid the pleasant chatter, grins, and handshakes filling the room, I watched Brandon's eyes. They continued to track me, but he wasn't moving his head. I recognized the heavy eyelids and the slow movements requiring focus and energy.

Remember that invisible force? FA is an energy deprivation disease, which means it doesn't take vacations. You start requiring more sleep but sometimes it's futile. You wake up in the morning already feeling exhausted. That feeling remains with you throughout the day.

It's most visible in the eyes, heavily lidded, working to fight off the persistent drag. If I try to open my eyes to look "normal," I feel awkward.

This exhaustion is built into the cause of the disease.

Friedreich's ataxia develops from a genetic marriage of man and woman—both parents must have a defective gene, and then there's a 25 percent chance that their child will have FA.

FA lives at the subcellular level. It manifests in the complex chemical relationships inside our cells. Genetic mutations happen when the sequencing on the strands of your DNA displays irregular patterns, when there are too many or too few, something's out of place, or there are excessive repeats of this or that.

People with Friedreich's ataxia have an excess repeat of a certain "nucleotide" sequence (GAA), which in most healthy individuals remains stable at thirty repeats or fewer. Above 100 repeats, it gets bad.

I have 450 repeats of GAA, which partly explains why my onset of FA occurred much later. Children with 1,000 repeats or more of GAA are in a wheelchair a lot earlier.

That's what pushes the urgency to slow the disease.

Research facilities like the Biodesign Institute are focusing their efforts on the mitochondria, where the genetic mutation for Friedreich's ataxia manifests its impact.

Omar Khdour, now a principal investigator in FA research at ASU's Biodesign Institute, explained that mitochondria are the powerhouse of the cells. They create energy. When we eat and digest food, the mitochondria take the nutrients and convert them to energy for the cell to function.

"Imagine putting gas in your car to run the engine," he says. "You step on the gas, the gas burns, the wheels run. You move down the street."

That's mitochondria at work.

When there's mitochondrial dysfunction, you still take in the food and nutrients, but they are not recognized or are mishandled, the car slows down, there's less energy, or the car runs in spurts and stops. Eventually, the engine fails.

With Friedreich's ataxia, a protein called frataxin sits at the center of this problem.

Frataxin's role is to assemble iron-sulfur clusters in the mitochondria to produce energy for cellular function in our body. Individuals with Friedreich's ataxia produce less frataxin, due to the genetic mutation. Less frataxin means fewer iron-sulfur clusters, and that means less energy produced by the mitochondria. It also means that iron is left over in the mitochondria because it is not assembled into a cluster to make energy.

This extra iron in the cell causes damage by acting as a "free radical," which causes oxidative damage to the cell. In the world around us, when iron oxidizes, it creates "rust" that reduces the functionality of moving metal parts—the rusty bicycle, the squeaky screw, or the stuck lock. Something similar happens inside our bodies when the mitochondria get "rusty."

That's how you end up with seventeen-year-old Brandon with his energy sapped, his movements compromised, his spine fused together, and the inevitable progression of a shortened life.

The Center for Bioenergetics, like many research institutes involved in FA research, works to lengthen life, while focusing on the dysfunction in mitochondria. Their approach is not to change the genetic mutation, but to slow the progression of the disease.

Some research has concentrated on trying to reduce the number of free radicals in the system, improving mitochondrial function, and/or increasing the amount of frataxin.

This agenda has led the Biodesign Institute on a path to develop drugs that could reverse the effects of mitochondrial dysfunction, with results that could potentially be applied to many modern diseases.

Although not a cure, any development to increase life expectancy creates hope for researchers like Omar Khdour, who meets mothers of five-year-old children asking, "Do we have hope?"

Without hope, Khdour says, there's no point to research.

Looking at Brandon, stiff in his wheelchair, I wanted to give him hope. I wanted him to feel like he was part of a solution. But I couldn't.

Meeting Brandon made me question how effective I could be. I didn't know how to reach out to him. I wanted to make a connection, but I felt powerless. I tried to act positive and upbeat, but we both felt trapped by the reality of the situation.

Once again, I questioned my role as "ambassador" to this disease, a familiar confusion that increased my lack of clarity. I didn't have the words—yet—to speak to a boy like this.

When disease hits you at a young age, you're forced to deal with realities that no ten-year-old should face. The disease hit me at seventeen, but not its total devastation. At least I was able to develop a sense of my physical body moving into my early twenties. Although I stumbled and fell and lurched, the disease hadn't fully defined me yet. On the other hand, I struggled to accept the reality of my situation, even as I rode across America.

I winced at the large monitor in the lobby which read: Welcome Kyle Bryant, Ride Ataxia. I felt proud, but I saw the sign through Brandon's eyes,

What's there to be proud of?

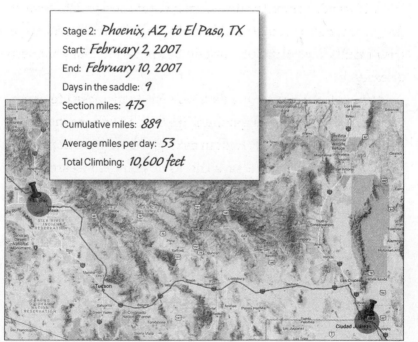

Stage 2: *Phoenix, AZ, to El Paso, TX*
Start: *February 2, 2007*
End: *February 10, 2007*
Days in the saddle: *9*
Section miles: *475*
Cumulative miles: *889*
Average miles per day: *53*
Total Climbing: *10,600 feet*

Map data ©2018 Google via ridewithgps.com.

RIDING ACROSS THE SURFACE
OF THE MOON

The next morning, as we pulled out of Phoenix and pointed toward the high deserts of the Southwest, I still wrestled with these ambiguities.

I thought about Brandon, sitting artificially erect in his wheelchair back at ASU. I felt helpless, unable to connect. I attempted to placate him and embarrassed myself in the process. Even in my condition, I was still part of the problem. I was trying to put on a happy face without a clear sense of direction.

As we pushed farther south on the highway, a wall of wind slammed into us. It lasted for miles, and then days, hitting us from every direction. I was forced to concentrate on the task at hand.

A windy day in the city is one thing. You walk down a sidewalk, across a parking lot, through a muddy park, then the wind picks stuff up, throws you back, bends trees. You duck for cover, move into the shelter of a building… wait it out. But in the desert you're totally exposed and this wind was a grinding, inconceivable force, like an invisible wall. I felt diminished by its power.

Fortunately, I was spurred by the addition of a childhood buddy, Andy Smith, who landed in Phoenix the night before, his bike in a box, ready to roll with us for a week. When we pulled out of the city, I was buoyed by his presence.

Andy was the first of many "guests" who would drop in for fifty or several hundred miles. These visitors became a powerful feature of my experience. They demonstrated that the success of this ride mattered to more people than just my family.

Andy understood me like no other friend. We had known each

other since elementary school, and we were college roommates. We could laugh for hours about nothing. He was also one of the first friends to whom I talked about my disease. It was a spontaneous and drunken statement of despair on the cement stairs outside our dorm room.

"I'm going to die," I blurted, my words echoing into the stairwell. "And I'm going to be in a wheelchair in the next few years."

Andy almost looked relieved. We were finally having a conversation. "Well, we're here for you, no matter what happens," he said.

I didn't realize how important it was to talk to my friends about my disease. I kept my feelings hidden. No doubt he felt inadequate in that moment as well.

When I invited him on the ride, it offered him a chance to do something. I think it made everyone feel that way, a way to contradict our powerlessness.

In the late afternoon, long after we left Phoenix glowing beneath the winter sun, we moved into a higher elevation. We had been riding in silence for many miles, passing through the southeast corner of Arizona, a high-altitude desert, sliding along 4,000-foot ridges, while dropping into deep valleys. Out of that silence Andy said: "You know. I've been screwing around in front of your parents my entire life. Now we're actually doing something that matters."

I laughed. "We're still screwing around," I said. "Now we're just doing it with purpose."

After we entered the San Carlos Apache Reservation, we were faced with a steep elevation increase and blind curves that made safe riding impossible. The situation stopped our entire forward momentum, and we decided to re-evaluate the Adventure Cycling maps. Our decision took us on a detour to Interstate 10, a short drive to the south. I was worried about dropping into high speed traffic, but I-10 had grown smaller and quieter, punctuated by a striking desert landscape with ancient red rocks, deep shadows, and a history, even darker. We rode into Sulphur Springs Valley and passed through Willcox, a quiet town of 3,000 inhabitants— beyond that, solitude stretched for hundreds of miles in every direction. Across the valley, stood the Chiricahua Mountains, with Chiricahua Peak rising to 9,759 feet.

Here the Apache Indians had lived, raised families, and subsisted off mountains and grassy plains, where mule deer, jaguars, fish, and other game sustained their culture for thousands of years. Just to the south sat Skeleton Canyon, where Geronimo had surrendered to thousands of troops and civilian militia in the late 1800s, officially ending the Indian Wars. The Apache resistance had been fierce, beginning with Cochise and eventually finalized with forced relocations to distant lands.

We rode over another rise and I could see thirty miles across the desert valley—no wagon trains, no troop movements, just barbed wire, tires in the brush, dry and barren, where the northern frontier of Mexico touches the southern edge of the United States.

It was like the surface of the moon, but a brown and red moon, with blue sky stretching above, the tangy smell of creosote brush and dirt. The wind whipped dust devils into circular funnels along the side of the road.

I shouted something pointless to my dad, like, "I'm hungry." He cupped his hand over his ear, shook his head, and hunched his shoulders, fighting against the brute force of a strong headwind.

Fortunately, I had a little advantage. Since a recumbent trike sits lower to the ground, theoretically I get less wind resistance. I'm able to push through the wind with a little less difficulty. This notion took a bit of the stress off my knee injury, which was becoming more problematic with each mile.

As we neared the shadow of Chiricahua Mountain, stacks of clouds towered above an eastern mountain range. Occasionally, they would block the sun, softening the landscape, and then the sun would reappear, casting long winter shadows.

For several days, we rode through this arid and dreamy terrain until finally we woke up with the wind at our backs.

THE MAGIC OF TAILWINDS

A tailwind is a helpful force. It's like you're in a bubble of support. The wind pushes into you from behind, like arms pushing you up a hill. As you move toward your destination, you get a boost.

If I pedaled hard enough to match the speed of the wind, I could hit 25 mph, which is my nominal speed on a downhill. I felt pulled and pushed simultaneously.

As long as we kept pace with the wind, we were in a sound tunnel, streaming across the landscape. I looked down at the road and watched the sand blowing in thin sheets that kept pace with my trike. I heard the click of the chain on the gears and watched a train pass in the distance, a quiet string of freight cars, sliding over the tracks at 50 mph.

While this magical buoyancy pushed me down the road, my thoughts returned to the Biodesign Institute, where I left Brandon and a team of scientists laboring over the mysteries of genetic code. I couldn't get my head around it.

How was that entire facility—with its tall windows, squeaky glass, shiny floors, advanced equipment, and state of the art scientists—supposed to find a cure for an inherited disease? How was that even possible? A genetic disease manifests like hair color, bone structure, foot size. You can dye your hair blond, but you still have brown hair. How can you "cure" eye color?

I get it. That specific institute is not trying to cure the disease, just slow its progression. But everybody speaks of a cure as if it's the panacea, the endpoint of the process. What happens during the in-between? We're so eager to reach for hope that we often forget the moments, the incremental steps along the way. The right now.

If you consider that a genetic disease is like your hair, your skin, or the shape of your nose, then you *must* consider other possibilities, thoughts that move you away from the paradigm of being victimized, thoughts that focus on the quality of your life. It can't be: *I'm going to live my life in spite of my disease.* Instead, it must be: *I'm not going to live my life in spite of anything.*

People with Friedreich's ataxia are prime examples of these possibilities. Already in a wheelchair, already unable to walk steadily across a room, already struggling with serious physical issues, needing assistance with bathing, dressing, eating, all the things we take for granted—they don't see themselves as sick. They don't view themselves as compromised.

These children I meet, as well as my family, my friends, and so many others who cross my path are the "tailwinds" in my life. They provide me with the buoyancy to pedal ahead, and offer a contradiction to a certain worldview.

When we become permanently married to the medical profession and its labeling of our disease, we surrender our capacity to determine our own fates. While doctors and researchers express compassion, the patient is often removed from the equation. We hear "disease" and "sickness" and "disability" and enter a long road of dependency upon a system that defines our world. Consequently, we spend far too much energy in despair.

We need to reach for emotional tailwinds in order to contradict this feeling. We need to reach for a prescription outside the concerns of our disease. Perhaps, as a result of my disease, I'm more tuned into this aspect, like a person who is blind and whose hearing improves. I want to make connections with people because I know this creates possibilities.

It allows me to tune into other considerations. What if this is who I am? Maybe disability is neither bad nor good.

It's just different.

Once we challenge the landscape of our language, we change our relationship to disease. We change other people's relationship to disease. We take steps to outpace despair and make different choices. We transform how we speak with our doctors, and with the people in our life, but, most important, we change the dialogue we have with ourselves.

When you clarify the situation and remind your doctors, care providers, or those who minister to your "disability" with words such as, "*Okay, I'm here, so how do I make the most out of my life … today,*" you're taking steps to reimagine a different future.

As the sun dropped over a red mesa, we pulled into the Alaskan RV Park in Bowie, Arizona, during the mid-afternoon. We planned to perform some routine maintenance on our bikes, which was really routine since we didn't know anything about bike maintenance. We started taking things apart, like wiping off accumulated grease, oiling the chain, cleaning the frame. It made us feel like we were doing something.

Several people passed and told us about the Sideman Music Festival, a popular event at the RV park. It happens every February and was founded by Judy Hall, who had toured as a backup singer with country greats like Merle Haggard, Waylon Jennings, and George Strait. Her intention was to create a venue where "sidemen" could take the center stage and perform as equals.

"Let's do it," my dad announced to the group with a raised brow. "But don't touch anyone...or anything."

We all fell silent. What did he mean?

"We don't want to bring back any outsider germs into our camp and jeopardize the trip," he said.

My mom rolled her eyes. "Seriously, Michael?"

My dad is not a germaphobe, but he always imagines the worst-case scenario—a result of his life as an insurance man. I knew he was half-joking because the first person he would meet, he'd stick out his hand.

Soon we ventured over to a large hall where we heard musicians warming up. As we drew near the crowd, I felt my dad move closer to me, which had become habitual whenever we were in large groups. He was always looking for a clear pathway because my stride was unpredictable. I staggered. I lurched. Sometimes, I fell.

People in the crowd noticed my unusual gait and stared. At that point in my life, I wasn't interested in holding onto someone's arm. My dad's solution was to hover in case I started to fall. He ignored gawkers. He didn't want to draw attention to my disability, not out of embarrassment but to encourage our right to experience a night out.

As the audience collected around the stage, I was swept into the Americana of the moment, joined by a bunch of elderly folks —snowbirds with their fully equipped RVs—and I forgot any feelings of inadequacy.

I loved the coincidence. We were watching some of the greatest country musicians and thinking to ourselves, "How did we end up here?"

The jam session lasted for several hours as Judy Hall—now a seventy-year-old matriarch who had recently released her latest album—ran around demanding her favorite songs from her musician friends, shouting encouragement, and singing along.

CROSSING THE RIO GRANDE
BENEATH A PERFECT BLUE SKY

After leaving Andy at the Tucson Airport, we pushed through the Arizona desert and reached the Rio Grande in record time. We ceremoniously crossed the river, which flows down out of Colorado alpine meadows and snakes through the arid territories of the American Southwest. It reaches the Gulf of Mexico, nearly 2,000 miles later, cutting through canyons and giving life to ecosystems along its boundary.

Much of the flat riverbed was bone-dry, but I could feel the abundance, the thriving life, after so many miles in a seemingly empty desert. We had reached a wide valley, where distant mountains with jagged peaks thrust out of the desert. We soon turned south, passing through Las Cruces, and rode through a fertile stretch of land with abundant pecan orchards, cottonwood trees, and modest commercial farms.

My fatigue and knee injury had intensified. The effort of the ride had pushed me to my limits. I felt a bone-tired certainty that spread through my body. This exhaustion had become a huge factor, more than the physical challenges of climbing hills, more than the endless stretches of road. I felt the weight of the consistent grind, which began to wear me down, in part due to the tedium of the hours, knowing we had weeks to go, but really it was the sheer physical effort that made things real.

I hadn't realized what I was getting into. Also, my sleep was lousy. Too many thoughts were spinning in my head. During the evenings I was arranging meet-ups with researchers and people living with FA. During the day, I was thinking about what I would write in my blog posts. I felt the numbers of the community following the ride, and a certain responsibility to maintain connection. As a result, I was anxious and irritable.

It wasn't necessarily about "fun" anymore. It was starting to be work.

Typically, when fatigue hits me on a ride, I feel like there's a quick fix, perhaps some food, or an energy bar, but at that point in the journey, nothing was going to fix me. My eyes were drooping. My mind grew increasingly blurry. My legs felt heavier with each mile.

The one saving grace was Highway 28, which was our current route to El Paso, Texas. It was a perfect road, smooth, quiet and fast, with one lane running in each direction. Most of the time, roads are bumpy, defined by rocks, gravel, cracks, bumps, aging ripples in the cement; curves, rises, dips, bottomless cliffs to one side. While my recumbent offered a bit of a comfort advantage to the two-wheeled rider, the physical fight with the road was constant.

On most roads, you have to imagine every conceivable opposition. During the long hours, I would lean back on the headrest, while at the same time my teeth rattled in my head; my hands vibrated on the handlebars; and my legs wobbled every time I crossed the rumble strip. Throw in the headwinds, traction, resistance, and gravity working to slow me down, and you get a constant, physical assault on the body.

But Highway 28 was a miracle.

No teeth rattling. No white knuckles. No wobbling legs. Just smooth and perfect, like riding across a recently polished basketball court. We passed country farms set back from the road and even a man who smiled at us from the perch of his tractor.

I started thinking about my brother, Collin, imagining that he would really dig our adventure. Not only the scenery, but the intensity of the ride. My brother loved physical challenges, and he had crazy endurance. We would ride mountain bikes when we were younger. My dad and I rode more frequently than Collin, but whenever he joined our rides, he would crush us, waiting at the top of each hill.

As the symptoms of my disease impacted my coordination —long before we knew I had a disease—the physical implications began to create distance between us. My diagnosis was still five years away, but the symptoms manifested in every area of my life.

When I was twelve years old, my dad, brother, and I would head to a secret fishing hole near the Feather River in Northern California. We spent hours hopping across river rocks. My dad and brother easily jumped from rock to rock, but my jumps required a series of steps. I'd jump to a rock, crouch, steady myself, then jump to another, teeter for a moment, then prepare for another leap, frequently slipping. I wanted to impress my dad and my brother. So, I pushed ahead while my dad grumbled, "Kyle, keep up," but the invisible force held me back.

After a long day, my exhaustion would peak, and my brother would be climbing trees and running around. I resented that at some level. *Why couldn't I keep up?* I wanted to be part of the team. I wanted to be a normal kid. But that wasn't going to happen.

As my symptoms grew worse, my limitations became the new normal. On one hunting trip, we planned an excursion to a duck blind. I really wanted to go along but at that point, everyone knew I couldn't navigate difficult terrain. My dad and brother figured out how to accommodate my trek. They had to borrow some-body's ATV, and when we reached the blind, they had to carry me across the knee-deep water because of the uneven ground and mud. Eventually, my appetite for those outings diminished.

As my dad and I pedaled through the Mesilla Valley toward El Paso, we were sharing a physical experience that I had wanted my entire life, but the reality of my total fatigue, accompanied by a serious knee injury, intensified my recall of those memories.

Who am I kidding? This is not something I was meant to accom-plish. And my brother's not around to carry me across the pond.

Somehow, leaving Arizona and inching our way toward the far corner of Texas made the trip more real and frightening. While my dad and I rarely spoke during long stretches, our silence became more profound. His exhaustion was peaking, as well. We were both hitting our limit.

Our speed slowed to a crawl by the time we reached my mom in the support vehicle for lunch. As I ate my tuna sandwich and sipped my V8 juice from the cushy bench of the trailer my eyelids got heavier and I slumped over into a deep sleep. There was no waking me, so my parents left me alone and drove the remaining ten miles to El Paso.

I slept until the next morning–eighteen hours of sleep.

That night, after our rest day, we ate dinner at a seafood restaurant (a strange concept in a desert town). The interior of the place was dark, with low hanging lamp fixtures, most of the décor a throwback to the 1970s. That alone should have served as a warning.

Within a few hours of the meal my dad said he was feeling sick, and proceeded to spend the entire night barfing in the trailer toilet. The food poisoning accompanied by sheer exhaustion took a serious toll on his body.

The next day, stoic as ever, pale-faced, and gaunt, my dad pulled on his bike gear and clipped into his pedals. I limped over to my recumbent and winced as I bent my knee into place.

We both hesitated to start off as we faced 900 miles of arid Texas landscape. Across the nearby border in Ciudad Juarez, a disorganized maze of grey urban housing tracts hugged the desert and dry foothills. I looked at my dad, and I knew what he was thinking. There's no way we can do this.

The sun burned through my cycling shorts as I grunted through the first pedal stroke.

CHAPTER 4

The One-Legged Man and the Ten-Year Walk for Jesus

magine reggae music on twenty cups of coffee. Then imagine about 200 high school and college kids, also fueled on twenty cups of coffee, jumping up and down, screaming.

That was me.

From the crowd, I'm watching a spiky-haired punk rocker on-stage, wearing a worn leather jacket, a set of low hanging chains from his waist, and high-top Chuck Taylors. He's grabbing fistfuls of his bass guitar to set the beat. The singer at his side shoves the microphone into his mouth, eyes wide as he leans close to the crowd, his black T-shirt emblazoned with a bleeding skull, which snarls at the audience. The guitarist jumps up and down, pounding on his electric guitar, shouting the undecipherable words to a familiar song.

The mosh pit is grinding near the stage where I'm standing, its epicenter is filled with bodies. The beat is intoxicating, the drive hypnotizing the entire room.

The infectious groove of ska punk music hits the walls of the club where my friends and I have converged on a weekend night. Everybody's going crazy, elbows and sweat and screaming into my ear, hair slapping me in the face, a knee in the groin. It's a rush of adrenaline, and I'm lost in the moment, anywhere from slightly panicked to laughing hysterically. Sometimes I can't move— perhaps I can flex my ankles a bit—but, as I press into the bodies around me, I struggle to keep my head high in order to breathe. Along the wall, a few of my friends are "skankin'," a dance that mimics the movement of a lizard skipping in place, where you lift opposite legs and arms, creating a slow-motion run.

When the "third wave" of ska punk hit the San Francisco Bay Area in the late 1980s and 90s, I was coming of age in Grass Valley, darting around the foothills of the Sierras, skiing, biking, hiking, lifeguarding, and wakeboarding at Lake of the Pines near our house.

When I got Green Day's first major label release, *Dookie*, for my birthday, I was hooked. I learned all the lyrics and rocked out to the infectious melodies. For a time, *Dookie* was the *only* CD I owned, but most of all, I loved attending shows in the suburbs of Sacramento and moshing with the rest of the crowd.

My friends and I would drive toward Sacramento to see local concerts. We took pride in driving to the smaller shows, where kids would crowd into little theaters and music stores to see bands like *The Brodys* or *Enemy You*. I was never into the political aspects of punk. I was attracted to its pure energy and rebellious spirit.

After my diagnosis, even though skankin' was a considerable challenge, I imagined a future that required loud music and rocking out. I wanted to feel like it wasn't over. I pictured myself at shows in a wheelchair. Since I couldn't get to the mosh pit, my friends would carry me on their shoulders, throw me onto the crowd, and I would crowd-surf.

It was an exhilarating image but at the same time the vision disturbed me. For a time, I was obsessed with that limited concept of myself, an idea that my future was reduced to small, measurable quantities. My imminent physical failures determined that future, like attending shows in a wheelchair or not being able to drive a car, overshadowed by a persistent self-doubt, a dread that infused my body every day. It's a debilitating perspective, one that infected me with fear. Millions of people experience a similar sensation— able-bodied or not. We're never good enough, smart enough, beautiful enough, kind enough, no matter how hard we try.

Self-doubt is the most dangerous drug on the planet.

Stage 3: *El Paso, TX, to Comfort, TX*
Start: *February 11, 2007*
End: *February 22, 2007*
Days in the saddle: *10*
Section miles: *500*
Cumulative miles: *1,389*
Average miles per day: *50*
Total Climbing: *14,000 feet*

Map data ©2018 Google via ridewithgps.com.

REACHING THE POINT OF NO RETURN

Fortunately, as my dad and I traversed a Texas country road pushing east of El Paso, my outdated beliefs were fading. Instead of a man forced to abandon an old life defined by athleticism and physical perfection, I could redefine myself in a new light, but not one that rejected my potential.

Once we passed the Colorado River, I had reached a point of no return. I wasn't going to feel limited. Maybe I couldn't execute a perfect ska dance. Maybe I couldn't close my eyes and head-bang without hitting the ground, but I was pedaling deep into an American desert on three wheels with the wind at my back, powered by two nearly functioning legs. This fact alone rewired my outlook, a view that saw life with a disability as diminished and irretrievable.

How could I continue to see myself as "disabled" when the opposite was true?

Dry desert air smacked into my face, and the wind pelted my skin with dust. In the distance, "sky islands" rose above the desert and my dad and I passed through a high-altitude basin in the Chihuahuan Desert. Our location placed us dead center of a vast geographic ecosystem. I could smell the wildness bearing down upon the earth.

Our ground level view was dominated by the pervasive creosote bush. It spread across the flat terrain in all directions. The Native Americans of the region believed that it held curative properties for tuberculosis, chickenpox, even snakebite. Maybe the bush would work for FA. Maybe the cure was a short miracle away. The entire desert felt that way: barren, yet holding mysteries and sudden possibilities. The World Wildlife Fund dubbed the Chihuahuan Desert one of the most biologically diverse ecoregions in the world, with much of that diversity thriving in the sky islands—isolated mountain ranges surrounded by lowlands. We had reached a confluence of desert and sweeping basins that revealed the massive geologic features of the Southwest, some of those basins running for hundreds of miles, which, in turn, infused me with a sense of the epic changes in my life.

On a purely physical level, any cyclist who has experienced the Southwest understands how to translate this vastness: gnarly wind.

I watched my dad pedal in front of me, head down, shoulders hunched, accelerating with shocking speed. A tailwind slammed into us from behind, flinging us across the grasslands. Dad was digging it. He was flying. He was smiling. He was having one of those mad dad moments.

Then the road turned and we fell victim to the annoying crosswind. But Dad had a solution.

As the wind roared, he grabbed the gust with one outstretched arm, and tacked across the road. Then he would lift the other arm and return to the other side. It was a cartoon moment, like watching a clown at the circus, the rider scooting and zigzagging across the two-lane road.

Most of the time, I wasn't entirely sure how my dad felt about the trip. He wasn't a big talker. Not strong on showing emotion. But as he zigzagged down the road, I witnessed a different man. A man filled with hope, the thrill of the ride, the spirit of adventure, whatever you want to call it. Instead of surrendering to the inevitable, he was grabbing the moment.

That's why imminent thoughts of failure terrified me. I didn't want to let him down. I didn't want this moment to end.

Since we left Arizona, the pain in my knee had become debilitating. Some mornings, we would hit the road, and I could hardly pedal. While I couldn't ignore the injury, I didn't want to give up, but it was a serious possibility.

After lunch that day (tuna fish sandwiches and V8)—a few hundred miles west of the Pecos River—we faced a gradual but steady uphill climb across the high-altitude landscape and the injury came to a head. I could no longer use my leg. With my left knee out of commission, my dad tried to push me up the hill, hoping that we would eventually reach a downhill for a few miles, but the hill didn't end. I tried to pedal farther, completing half a stroke with my right foot and then back pedal for half a stroke, trying to ratchet along, but I couldn't ride an inch. We decided to call my mom, who had driven twenty miles ahead to set up camp for the night, but our cell phones didn't have reception.

When I reached into my pocket to try calling again, it was empty. We all understand the extreme despair that accompanies the loss of our cell phones. But technology was our lifeline on the road. After I found shelter beneath an underpass, my dad rode back into a 40-mph headwind to look for the phone. He returned forty-five minutes later. No phone. He decided to ride ahead twenty miles to our campground.

After he left, I pedaled with my one good leg to a rest stop along Interstate 10, hoping I could borrow somebody's phone. I approached a man in a semitruck who spoke little English. Since he didn't have a phone, he offered his CB radio, which was useless.

I approached another couple and asked if I could borrow their phone. "Sorry, we're Canadian," the woman said.

"Canadians don't use cell phones?" I asked.

They eyed me suspiciously, a fully bearded young man riding a tricycle with one working leg in the middle of nowhere. They had no intention of letting me use their phone, so I returned to the underpass and waited several more hours.

Eventually, our support vehicle arrived and we retraced our tracks to find the phone in the gravel next to the road where I had made a call and apparently didn't zip it back into my pocket.

The experience reveal two things: 1.) Always zip your pocket after using the phone; 2.) I had to figure something out for my knee, or the adventure was over.

That night at Van Horn RV Park, I couldn't walk. My dad had to carry me to the bathroom, so I could take a shower. The pain had become unbearable, and we needed a solution.

I remembered Clint, a friend who lived in Midland, Texas, only a few hours away by car. I met him at an Ataxia conference a few years earlier. So I called him to ask if he could recommend a doctor. The next morning, we drove two hours up to Midland, where Clint got me an appointment with a local sports doctor.

"Yup, your knee is injured," the doctor said. He didn't want to give me another cortisone shot because I was a young guy and it might promote further injury.

But the doctor's visit wasn't a total loss. While we sat in the waiting room, Clint and his father Dave arrived. Their appearance was fortuitous. I had been looking for a machine shop to make some knee-saving trike modifications suggested by my uncle Steve, who was joining us in San Antonio. And Clint's father Dave happened to manage a nearby machine shop.

My knee wasn't going to miraculously heal, so my choice was stark: Quit the ride or modify the crank.

In Odessa, a team of technicians greeted us inside the cavernous shop. This was no small-town mechanic's garage. Enormous machines filled space under tall industrial ceilings, winter light filtering through the high windows; the smell of oil and grease, as chains and pulley systems swung from the ceiling to support heavy equipment. Outside, big trucks echoed into the muffled interior of the shop as they backed their rigs into enormous loading docks.

A team of soft-spoken men with Southern drawls stared down

at my fire-red recumbent. It looked vulnerable, parked there on the grease-stained floor. We discussed options. We scratched our beards.

One of the mechanics pointed to the crank and said, "That's a tiny piece of metal."

Another one said: "Yep."

"I'd like to take it for a spin," a third said.

"You'd fall over," needled a fourth.

It was like we were talking about a horse race or the weather. There was something unhurried about the whole affair, but at the same time no one doubted it was a problem that needed urgent attention.

Rich Fuston was the senior service manager. He was a tall man with a slow drawl.

"Kyle, the machinist can drill and tap a new hole in the crank, allowing us to situate the pedal closer to the center," he said, "and you'll have a shorter crank."

He pointed out a big problem: My trike used metric hardware and the threads on the left crank were reversed. Not only did the shop *not* have a metric tap—since all the machinery was standard size—it was going to be impossible to find a reverse-threaded metric tap.

The right pedal was "forward" threaded, so if we had two right pedals, we might have a solution.

We set out in search of a local bike shop to buy another set of pedals so we could have two rights, while the machine-shop technicians called around to find a metric tap. We found a bike shop, bought a crank puller, a pedal wrench, a new set of pedals, and a spare crank in case our plan didn't work.

When we got back to the shop, they had found a metric thread tap at a local supply store. We pulled the crank and they drilled the hole, but it was too small. Someone drove to Sears to fetch the right-sized bit. After about five hours, we got the pedal to fit into the threads, effectively shortening the crank.

Clipping into the pedal was a challenge. Now my recumbent had two right-hand pedals so I had to turn the cleat on my left shoe backward. For the rest of the trip, my dad would have to physically insert my cleat into the pedal and click it into place for me. The entire crew surrounded my trike on the floor of the shop. I sat down and we clipped my foot into the pedal. I back-pedaled a few times. The left crank rotated, but, as a result of the reduced distance, my left knee hardly moved.

Success.

Now I just had to figure out how to pedal to Memphis on one leg.

As we packed up, we said our goodbyes and tried to convey how much this meant to us. Rich Fuston said, "Just be sure you make it to Memphis. We are rooting for you."

With a fixed crank and renewed resolve, drove back to Van Horn, where we had diverted from our original route. On the return, the sky darkened and snow drifted across the prairie. The flakes swirled and fell down over the wide expanse. I zipped my jacket and stared out the window, considering the past several days.

I could have pushed—stubbornly—and further damaged my knee, ending any chance at completing the journey. Instead, I chose to think objectively, without shrinking from a serious obstacle. After I circumvented my sense of failure, we figured out how to make things work.

When you remain objective in problem-solving, you remove

fear. If you focus on the problem, then you arrive at a solution and consider productive strategies.

And a second factor resurfaced: At every point along this journey, the right people kept showing up. I was reminded repeatedly that I was not alone.

The men at the Odessa machine shop were total strangers who took five hours in the middle of their workday to help contribute to the FA community. I thought about Clint and his dad, who just showed up and became instant allies. I thought about our old family friends, Wally and Mary Krill, who were about to catch up to us at a Van Horn campground. They drove their RV from Grass Valley to provide support and add a second SAG vehicle for the duration of the trip. Both octogenarians, they loved the call to adventure. They had completed many long-distance rides around the world on a tandem earlier in their lives.

We had also arranged a lunch in Van Horn with a group at the United Methodist church. Pastor Linda Mizzel, who had friends affected by FA, invited our growing team to meet with the congregation. And in a few days, we would rendezvous in Fort Stockton with the Neylands, Linda's friends who had lost their daughter Betsy to FA.

The scale of the experience humbled me, not because of my own grandiose accomplishments, but because of the web of humanity that emerged from the shadows, individuals extracting themselves from their suffering with the clear intention of doing *something*.

Back in Van Horn, my dad and I were eager to get on the road. While we waited for Wally and Mary to arrive, we decided to put in twenty or thirty miles to try out the new crank.

When we first dropped our bikes on the road, storm clouds appeared from the west—thick, black clouds accompanied by heavy wind, and after a hundred yards of riding into the wind, the clouds cracked open and poured hail like crazy. We turned around and retreated back to the safety of the trailer.

As soon as the hail stopped, we tried again. Fortunately, we brought our cold-weather cycling gear. Facing our first storm of the ride, we were excited to use our gear—waterproof jackets, rain pants, wool socks, neoprene booties over our cycling shoes, gloves, and special beanies that fit under our bike helmets.

It's hard to find the right balance in cold weather. Often your body is sweating, but your extremities are frozen. If the balance is off, riding can be miserable. When I would get overheated and frozen simultaneously, I reminded myself that I was out here riding a bike in the middle of nowhere, and I felt less miserable.

Compounding our fight with the weather, I had to adjust to riding with a shortened crank. Since my left knee was still useless, I couldn't use my left leg for power. I could only manage some pull.

We rode against a strong headwind. We couldn't get over 8 mph. We passed oil pumpjacks working like grasshoppers at the ground, dusted with snow. The steel machines punctuated the landscape, and exposed the smell of the ground seepage that permeated the air. A seascape of shrub stretched across the horizon beneath a black sky as we road along a generous shoulder. The wind was so loud we couldn't hear the approach of any cars or trucks. I focused on the road ahead.

Several hours into the ride, I saw him.

He was a vision of epic and historical proportions—a man dragging an eight-foot cross down a desolate Texas road. The man leaned into the wind, dragging his cross along the frontage road, which ran along the side of the highway. He wore a backpack, jeans, a Mexican serape partially covered by a plastic trash bag to keep it dry, and a baseball cap.

A few miles ahead, we reached the end of our mileage for the day, and waited for Wally to collect us in the support vehicle. After we described the man to Wally, we circled around. Wally was beside himself. Ever since we told him the story about the half-naked bookseller, he had wanted to join us on the trip. His bushy eyebrows jumped up and down as we pulled alongside the spiritual traveler.

Wally was the first to jump out of the car in order to greet the man.

"Hey, where are you traveling from?" he shouted over the wind.

The man's answer blew away in the wind, but then he hefted the cross onto his shoulder and said, "I'm walking for Jesus."

"Quite a heavy load," I said, nodding at his cross.

"Nope," he said, shaking his head. "It's hollow."

He rapped his knuckles on the side of the cross, which also had a wheel at the bottom for easier pulling.

He was Charles Johnson. God had instructed him to travel from Anaheim, California, down to Mexico with $55 in his pocket. The Lord also told him to find a carpenter who could build him a "mobile" cross, suitable for pulling across a continent. So, when the cross was finished, Charles left Mexico with two dollars in his pocket and began his decade-long walk-for-Jesus.

"So far, I've been walking for seven years," he told us, "just stopping and talking to people about Jesus. Every day, I say the same thing. 'All right Jesus. What now?' And I keep on walking."

He asked us for a ride to Pecos, Texas, but we were driving the opposite direction, so he just hefted his cross to his shoulder and walked on. Six months later, an article in a Pennsylvania newspaper proved he was still walking around the country, pulling his cross.

One might think, *Wow, that's one crazy dude.* But at least he wasn't a middle-aged man sitting on a couch, watching television, thinking about lost life. He was man following a dream, one that involved dragging an eight-foot cross around the country.

How was I any different? The only difference was my dream involved riding a tricycle.

When you're diagnosed with FA, you hear things like, "You'll be in a wheelchair soon. You'll lose the ability to take care of yourself. You will likely die a premature death due to heart disease."

Then you begin to meet people who choose to navigate an alternate reality. If you pay attention, you'll learn how others deal with life's challenges…and overcome them. You'll learn about the trauma that accompanies lives of hardship. But you'll also learn that your disease—or disability—is not a death sentence, and if you choose, you can walk through a world that will open your eyes to incredible things.

CHAPTER 5

Following Your Dreams? Prepare for Roadkill, High Winds, and the Stench of Oil

'Il tell you what I've learned: Texas is big.

Big country. Big hats. Big cars. Big sky. Big steaks. You name it.

Then there's the roadkill.

I've been riding my recumbent trike across 500 miles of desert for a week, and for the past 25 miles, I've passed more roadkill than a man needs to see in a lifetime. Yesterday on the highway, my dad and I passed about twenty-five dead deer, which turned the highway shoulder into an obstacle course.

How much roadkill can you get excited about? There's another dead deer. And another.

We were also fighting the wind—a wind you can't believe—pushing into an opposing force without much payoff. It wears you down hour after hour, slipping into every crevice and fold of your body.

There's so much wind, in fact, that I'm pedaling as hard as my one good leg will go. I'm pushing but not moving. I'm accelerating but it feels like I'm drifting backward. My speedometer reads 3 mph. At my output, I should be hitting seventeen mph. The force keeps pushing me back—a relentless, overpowering wave.

This kind of wind is an unknown quantity. You can't see it. You can't track its movement. You can only feel it as it kicks sand in your face.

In front of me, Dad's not moving either. His eyes are focused on the road and he's streamlined his body to reduce resistance. He looks like he's standing still.

You'd be surprised at the debris that collects on a desert highway. Throw in hurricane force winds, and you've got dead birds, strips of big rigs' torn tires, scraps of farm equipment, tumbleweeds, and drifts of sand. You've got microscopic rocks and dust pelting your face. Of course, there are the dead deer, snakes, and armadillos. All you can do is navigate and hope for the best.

Meteorologists confirm that this region of the U.S. gets the highest convection and most severe storms as anywhere in the world—something to do with the warm Gulf of Mexico, the Rockies, and the high plains creating the perfect conditions for severe weather.

We might not have been moving very fast, but the big rigs, ripping past with their 500 horsepower engines, tore the shirt off my back. I couldn't hear them until they were right next to me. They emerged from the dusty highway, first a small dot, a wavering heat signature, and then towering above me for a split second—80,000 pounds of rubber and steel and cargo, blasting our socks off.

I'd catch a glimpse the drivers' faces in my mirror, with their ball caps and tired eyes, leaning into the landscape, feeling the speed, perhaps the enormity of their journey. Their eyes focused on some distant thought, delivering cattle or tomatoes or grain or gasoline or light bulbs to the far reaches of the country.

When you consider the geography of land mass, the wide prairies, dry riverbeds, and jagged peaks, the scale reframes your place on the planet. Then if you place yourself on a road that traverses that land mass—Lycra shorts and a jacket as your only buffer—you've got the makings of an epic journey.

That morning at the RV park, I stepped out of our trailer and watched thunderstorms gather in the distance. A thin line of mountains defined the horizon, where a layer of clouds dumped rain onto flat peaks and hidden mesas covered with miles of prairie grass.

I could smell the moisture, rolling across the plains a hundred miles out. I felt the movement of land, like watching an ocean filled with whales, as they surfaced and lumbered beneath an endless sky. This physical hardness, its vastness softened by pastel edges, seemed like a mouth that could swallow me whole, lure me into a bleak world where I would never return.

With FA there's always going to be an external power in my life, a force that acts with impunity. Whether I'm faced with a disease, an inevitable life sentence, or a desert wind blowing across a landmass, I have to learn how to face those conditions.

I struggled to accept this simple fact. I wanted to ignore my predicament, deny its existence, but it kept coming. No matter how much I tried to reject the presence of my disease, it kept coming. Every time I resisted its certainty, it kept coming.

I'd like to say, a solution manifested beneath that Texas sun, but it didn't. I'd like to say that I was ready to meet this force head-on. But I wasn't. I'd like to announce the growth of imminent purpose. But it didn't happen.

I still had no idea what the hell I was doing, but I was doing something.

Yesterday, we passed the turn-off to Marlow, where actor James Dean shot *Giant*, his last movie. He died soon after when his Porsche 550 Spyder slammed into a Ford Tudor sedan on a California country road south of Salinas. It's a great detour, that rolling highway through California hills, with cows and oak trees, farms and valleys—but apparently too narrow for a high-powered German race car and an American clunker.

Starring Rock Hudson and Elizabeth Taylor, *Giant* allowed James Dean his last opportunity to play another tragic, disaffected youth. And Dean played the part to perfection. His character defied the expectations of the day—to get a job, settle down, tow-the-line, and shut your mouth.

Although it didn't end well for the character in the movie, I wasn't going to live the rest of my life by towing the line either.

As we powered on toward Fort Stockton, I watched the horizon. In West Texas, the locals say you can see clear into next week. When you have a terminal disease—whether a few months or years to live—you are given a gift of vision. You can view the endpoint. *You can see clear into next week.* It can be a blessing and a curse. You've been given the license to commit to your life, but if you're careless, you'll miss the moments when the wind stops and changes direction, and you fail to see opportunities where magical things happen.

When I received my diagnosis, the invisible force became visible, but it took me several years to figure out how to navigate that force. I kept looking ahead, attending too much on the deficit.

I was about to meet a family that would remind me to think differently.

When we reached Fort Stockton, we rendezvoused with locals who had been tracking our ride. We met at a Mexican restaurant for lunch in the middle of the tiny town. In the group were Ruth and Emily Neyland. The Neyland family had experienced the worst of Friedreich's ataxia. Both children, Betsy and Emily, were diagnosed with FA quite young. Betsy, the oldest daughter, died at the age of twenty-five. Betsy's younger sister Emily, wasn't diagnosed until she was twelve, and by the time we met, her symptoms were advanced.

Diagnosis for a rare disease can be a long journey. In the beginning, doctors just eliminate possibilities because they have no idea what's causing the symptoms. Before the gene was discovered in 1997, there was no conclusive, black-and-white test.

"They didn't do blood tests back then," says Emily. She had a vague memory as a child when she was tested. "They did something where we would lay on our backs, and they would have these long needles and they would poke them into my stomach, and measure our nerve reactions or something." Whether she describes an accurate procedure or not, her memory reveals the ambiguous nature of the diagnostic process at the time.

It was primitive, and it illustrates how families, like the Neylands, moved through a medical system that offered few definitive answers.

Eventually, Emily's blood tests came back positive for FA. Ten years later, she lives in a wheelchair full-time, struggling with the physical complications of FA. But when her sister died, she was left to face the disease alone.

Betsy's mother and sister shared stories about her life. They remember her as a young woman who had been determined to embrace life as long as possible.

"Betsy had this habit in high school," says Ruth, her mom. "She'd throw herself out of her wheelchair so the cute boys could pick her up and put her back in. When her dad took her to an NSYNC concert up in El Paso, she ran her motorized wheelchair into NSYNC's bus."

Betsy was a woman I would have liked to meet.

I knew a wheelchair was in my future. A time would come when I would transition to a wheelchair full-time, but I wanted to defy convention. I imagined wheeling myself into markets where I would pull up to the counter and stand up onto my feet in order to pay. I wanted to witness those moments when the cashier's confused face would say *Hallelujah! The man can walk!*

"Disabled" people deal with those preconceptions every day. We begin to believe we *are* limited, that our "possibilities" are finite. This kind of thinking cements a persistent feeling of defeat. But there are other possibilities, novel concepts to most "able-bodied" people.

Imagine if we took limitations off the table? Imagine if "disabled" was just a set of circumstances that needed some modifications. You'd have "disabled" people on the moon, wheelchair-bound athletes rounding the bases at Wrigley Field, and blind drivers motoring through the city streets.

When you remove *measurement* from the concept of ability, then you're left with people accomplishing what they can within their own framework. When we're allowed to initiate from our own unique beginning point, we can all perform at our optimal potential.

As I pushed beyond Fort Stockton, crossing the barren country past the oilfields and the rolling hills where the elevation gave way to the sea-level terrain of the Gulf, I could feel the extended FA family—Chelsea, Brandon, Clint, Betsy, Emily—making a clear choice not to remain invisible.

When we reached Sonora, we touched the heart of the old Wild West. This is where the shooting of William "News" Carver in Jack Owens' Bakery in 1901 grabbed national headlines. Carver was a gun-toting member of Butch Cassidy's Wild Bunch, robbing trains and shooting up saloons—a gangster who helped immortalize the sheen of the gunslinger.

We also visited Sonora's famed underground caverns, which offered a vast cave system of dripping rock—*speleothems* (mineral deposits formed from limestone), along with stalactites, stalagmites, and helictites—the formations hanging over our heads, each drip adding another layer of sediment that would last thousands of years.

These detours added to the backdrop of my experience, where the changing scenery deepened my connection to the road, to the country, and to the people we met along the way. I traveled across the expanse, reminded that the stories and myths and mountains and prairies of our country have always immortalized lives in a larger context, where the intrepid traveler takes risks and pursues a dream.

I was allowed to experience that path from the seat of my trike, where everything is circumstantial—the wind, the sun, the texture of the road, how much sleep you get—so you're allowed to focus on the immediate, what's needed, and where to go. This practice of attending to the moment can inform every action of an individual who faces a disease.

As we pushed deeper across that American frontier, my old life began to recede. My needs, my cravings, the insecurities, and desires grew less potent. Even though I was driven to exhaustion every day, I felt buoyed by something larger. Each night, when I sat down at the computer to post to my blog, make connections, or plan "meetups," I plugged into a greater community.

During the day, while I pedaled, I spent a significant amount of my brain power planning my blog posts for the evening. I started blogging eight months before the ride launch, and the responses began to pour in. The comments that I received inspired me to write more and document as much of the trip as I could. As I rode, I would build the narrative in my head. When you write a blog, you hope that somebody reads it. You send it out into the black hole of the Internet. The comments reaffirmed that people believed in the trip and created concrete evidence that we were making an impact.

My context had grown. The ride was no longer about me. My tunnel vision was making room for the incredible relationships in my life—my family, my friends, new connections, and the extended FA community.

I could feel the collective effort behind me. I could feel people stepping forward who wanted to do *something*. And the volume was increasing on a voice that needed to extend its range.

We weren't just striving for a cure. We were learning how to connect the threads, linking a network of individuals who wanted to build an identity beyond our disease, and beyond the limitations of a complacent worldview.

CHAPTER 6

The Queen of Walmart

As we advanced our mileage across the United States, our numbers began to grow. Along with Wally and Mary Krill, who added an additional RV to the lineup, we were powering toward San Antonio to pick up my uncle, who jumped at the opportunity to join us. The next day, a father and son team would arrive from Trophy Club, Texas, the two David Henrys, the younger David dealing with an unidentified form of ataxia (he would add a second recumbent to the mix).

But leading the charge was my mom, peering over the steering wheel of our Dodge Durango, avoiding the occasional ground squirrel or steering around unidentifiable roadkill.

When my mom signed on for the duration of the cross-country trip, she worked as a kindergarten teacher at Maria Montessori Charter Academy in Rocklin, California. With my diagnosis, her life turned upside down. She would leave work in the middle of the day, thinking terrible thoughts. Her visions—my life in a wheelchair, unable to feed myself, losing my ability to communicate—occupied her mind.

She began to reach out to a larger community, which was driven by other mothers who sought answers. Most of the letters and emails I receive come from mothers, who appear in great numbers at meetings, conventions, and fundraising efforts.

I've heard this story many times:

My son is fourteen years old, and he spends most of his time in a wheelchair. He can still walk, but he doesn't want to move. He feels like there's no point. He's angry all the time. His "friends" have vanished. No one seems to call him. He doesn't want to attend school. I don't know what to do.

When I suggested the cross-country ride, my mom was the first to pack a bag. She was the first to view the trip as an antidote to my family's helplessness. For a mother, the arrival of a neuro-degenerative disease hits like a catastrophic force. They understand the magnitude of the disease. They understand its potential to tear a family apart. My mom wanted to change this narrative. Instead of embracing uncertainty—a worldview that dominated our lives—the anticipation of a cross-country ride introduced an alternative view, one that embraced hope.

Since my mom was fully employed, she took a leave of absence from her job. Eight months after our meal at Outback Steakhouse, my mother jumped behind the wheel of our new 2007 Dodge Durango (a woman who had absolutely no experience pulling a large trailer) and roared away from the cliffs of La Jolla, California.

My dad and I pedaled along, leaning into the elements, facing the wind and the far reaches of the American frontier, but my mom was the force that kept us going.

As she navigated across the continent, she competed with heavy winds, a loaded trailer, and menacing trucks. The Durango was slightly underpowered for our haul, and we hadn't corrected our tongue weight with a distribution hitch, so the nose of the truck pointed skyward, and made it more difficult to navigate. At night, our headlights illuminated billboards, highway signs, and bats—but rarely the road.

Between making tuna fish sandwiches for lunch and setting up camp for the night, my mom had hours to kill. While my dad and I took the entire day to cover 50 miles, my mom cleared the distance in an hour. Rather than sitting around waiting for us to complete the mileage, she stopped at every Walmart between California and Memphis. She had her hair done, her nails painted, bought local art, supplies, looked at magazines, and had the oil changed. Along the road, she even bought bracelets, hats, and trinkets for friends.

But when she bought a three-foot copper palm tree (it really looked like a giant cookie cutter), I went crazy.

I felt that messianic importance that only a twenty-five-year-old can feel—*we're on a mission; we're raising awareness for a rare disease; we're leading an unseen community toward a cure*—and my mom was pushing a shopping cart through local Walmarts, wondering which town had a yarn store.

It agitated my sense of mission, and I made sure to let her know.

We had pulled over at a rest stop for lunch and ate our sandwiches in the trailer. I got up from the table and passed the closet.

When I saw a large metal object sticking out from beneath the coats, I knew it was her most recent purchase.

I pulled back the edge of a coat and glared. "Mom, are you kidding? How could you buy this…thing?"

She sat on the dining bench near the window, which faced the parking lot where travelers exited cars with their families and dogs and road-weary faces.

"It's a unique piece of art, Kyle," she said, shrugging her shoulders and admiring the thin, stressed copper like she was evaluating an artifact. "I bought it at a roadside stand. Isn't it cool? It can go on the wall in Collin's old room."

The cookie cutter had no place on a cross-country ride. I tried to sound authoritative.

"We need to execute our plan, Mom. How does this palm tree contribute to that?"

I was so focused on the end goal that every action had to support my objective, but it all came down to our unique coping style. While my mom's strengths drew from living in the present, I was trying to think ahead. I wanted to anticipate each step along the way, and sometimes the trip brought out the worst in me.

"I don't think we're on the same page," I blurted, and sat down.

The palm tree disrupted my idea of strategy. First, we bike here, camp there, eat up ahead, take a side detour, and connect with the research community. Then we wake up and do it over again. Eventually, we get to where we're going.

No three-foot copper palm trees. Period.

That's the divergence between a long-term thinker and someone who lives in the present. When the two meet on the road, someone's bound to get smacked down, and, of course, that someone was me.

Weighing my reaction, my mom placed a hand on her chest and pretended to catch her breath; her eyes grew wide, and she looked directly at my dad: "Michael, do you hear this boy?" Her tone was sarcastic, but the sarcasm reflected her firm grip on the situation. She anticipated my response, thus hiding the palm tree beneath a pile of coats because she was aware of the big picture.

My dad rolled his eyes and remained silent. He wasn't going to get involved.

My mom squinted at me and said, "I'll tell you what Kyle B. I'm going to pick your ears."

Since I was a child, she was obsessed with keeping my ears wax-free. My earliest memories involved my mom chasing me down with her manicured fingernails. As I grew older, her warnings began with a sternly pointed finger. She'd bring her outstretched finger close to my face and stare with one eye closed down the length of her arm like she was pointing a sword.

We sat at the table with our tuna fish sandwiches and cans of V8 juice, listening to the traffic as it passed along Interstate 10. My mom brought her long nail to my face, and I stared down at the purple polish. She wore her cooking apron with a bike embroidered across the chest. As she leaned toward me, I started to sweat.

Suddenly, I was six-year-old Kyle staring up at my mother, a mixture of fear and anticipation on my face. I thought *Is she really going to do this?* She rendered me powerless, and I ducked and quickly pulled myself out of the seat. "Michael. What's wrong with this boy, anyway?" she said.

My dad intervened: "Well, let's get back on the road," he mumbled, avoiding the drama. I said something about checking the bikes and staggered out the door.

After we mounted our bikes and pulled away from the rest-stop, my brain felt overheated. I was still angry about the situation. I took the concept—"we're all in this together"—seriously, the belief that accompanies families within rare disease communities. You hear parents say, "*We* have FA," not *my son or daughter has a disease.*

Just as families share the genetics of a disease, they often share its burden. It's the result of a consummation between two adults, random carriers of a defective gene. Perhaps one child in the family gets the disease. Perhaps all. Obviously it's nobody's fault, but everyone feels the blame.

Soon, I would transition to a wheelchair. Soon, I would lose more functions. Soon my disabilities would progress, and I was convinced we were all responsible for the inevitability of my decline.

I thought if my parents *didn't* help me, they were limiting me. *I'm holding up my end, you should hold up your own.* I knew this

Stage 4: *Comfort, TX, to Kinder, LA*
Start: *February 23, 2007*
End: *March 5, 2007*
Days in the saddle: *8*
Section miles: *411*
Cumulative miles: *1,800*
Average miles per day: *51*
Total Climbing: *12,100 feet*

Map data ©2018 Google via ridewithgps.com.

expectation was not logical. I knew the whole idea of the bike ride was unreasonable, but this situation defied logic, so I held onto the last shreds of this belief.

Still, I was the lucky one.

As the family member with the disease, I experienced some self-determination. I was forced to learn how to react to the facts of my disease, and make choices. I learned how to navigate my new world by trial and error. Parents don't have that option. They are a step removed, and as much as they would like to, they can't fix the disease. They can't just give their son or daughter a Tylenol, fluff the pillow, and say it will be better tomorrow. They have to watch, and wait, feel despair and helplessness.

While I pedaled toward San Antonio to rendezvous with my uncle, I kicked myself for assigning blame to my mom, but in that moment, I couldn't help myself. The arrival of two additional riders, however, began to shift that perspective.

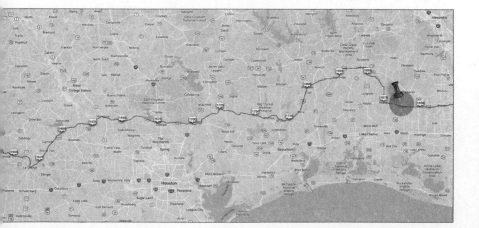

SHIFTING GEARS THROUGH
TEXAS HILL COUNTRY

Two days later, after departing from I-10 near Comfort, Texas, as we rode north of San Antonio, we pedaled *en masse* into the rolling hills of Texas, our adventure now defined by two additional riders—my Uncle Steve and one of the David Henrys. Our route took us north away from Interstate 10, along a rural "farm to market" road.

In the United States, farm-to-market roads were created in the 1930s to bring the farmer to the city ("get the farmer out of the mud"). The government wanted to connect rural and agricultural areas to urban centers. Texas had a lot of country and not a lot of road, so the Texas Department of Transportation built a network of these roads, adding to more than half the state's highway mileage.

For the cross-country cyclist, you get a paved highway, but not a superhighway. The disadvantage arrived in the absence of a shoulder—we had to watch our backs and practice defensive cycling.

As we transitioned into Texas Hill Country, we passed country barns and tangled stretches of bald cypress, Spanish oaks, and sycamore trees growing like weeds along deep creek beds. We passed lush meadows and white-tailed deer crossing in the distance while red-tailed hawks circled above.

The extra riders and another family member diminished my isolation. Uncle Steve didn't see me as a disabled man. He saw me as an athlete, and he took my goals seriously.

David Henry, with his clinical diagnosis of ataxia, held up another kind of mirror. Here was a man, who wanted to prevail against his circumstances, while accepting the features of his new life. I still didn't see myself as a man with a disease. I didn't picture myself as part of that group. When David joined us for the ride, I was able to view my existence from another perspective. His continual presence over the next week allowed me to put my toe in the water, then my entire foot. I could see David as an individual, and I could observe his disabilities, and while the two were connected, one did not depend on the other. Perhaps it was possible to consider myself as someone who could exist separately from my disability.

David's presence also provided me with an opportunity to measure up against another rider. I wanted to prove my strength, and David normalized the curve. We were both facing the inevitability of our physical decline, and we both were forced to work within our limitations.

On the other hand, my uncle's presence introduced an entire menu of contexts to observe. I respected how he managed adversity in his life. He arrived with a well-used mountain bike, a loose gear cluster, new road tires, and a reconstructed knee. He lived in Libby, Montana, where he'd worked through the years as a chef, ran a restaurant, a gas station, and a natural foods store, then onto logging, and "pulling chain" at the lumber mill. Life had not always been so easy. He drank, started fights, generally made a mess of things, until one day his daughter said, "Daddy, I don't like it when you're drunk."

He went cold turkey and remained sober for seventeen years.

After his knee replacement, he broke his femur while mountain biking. Back to the hospital, a few more metal rods, and several months without bending his new knee. From that point, his knee only bent to about 80 degrees. In order to continue riding his bike, he shortened the crank on the left side. That's how I got the idea to shorten mine.

Conscious of his enduring injuries, he turned into a strategic athlete, and he took his endeavors seriously. After each day of riding, he wrote down our mileage, took notes and recorded everything in a ragged spiral notebook. He had developed this habit over the years, writing the details of every athletic undertaking —how many days skiing, hours at the gym, time on the rowing machine, mountain bike rides, and hiking. After he completed his notes, he would thumb through the notebook like a magazine and compare the day's ride to last year or the year before.

David Henry joined our team with his Greenspeed GT5 Trike. I had never ridden with another trike before, and we were both excited to try drafting with our three-wheelers.

Typically, when two or more cyclists ride together, the wind force can be reduced when one rider rides closely behind another (drafting). The front rider bears the brunt of any headwind and determines the pace, giving the second rider a break from the wind. Since my dad rode an upright, there was no advantage to drafting behind him.

The extra riders also added to the momentum of the ride. On the first morning, after we dropped our bikes and recumbents on the road, I was pumped. I wanted to push myself (not a great plan, since I was largely pedaling with one leg), and riding with another recumbent triggered my competitive nature.

We rolled into a long stretch of hill country, where nine-banded armadillos and rabbits roamed the undergrowth. The smell of moisture and heavy vegetation hung over the woods, and long stretches of loblolly pine lined the shallow canyons and spread along the hills. The steep rises offered a serious challenge to my injured knee, as the highway turned into a roller coaster. That's when David and I decided to make our first attempt at drafting.

We faced a slight uphill with the wind on our faces, and I let David pass. I understood the concept of drafting, but I was a novice, and if I got too close, we could both end up in the dirt. As I neared his back tire, the wind force dropped, and I felt butterflies in my gut. The strategy worked and I experienced the magic of physics. Less resistance, more output. My sore legs benefited, as well, from the reduced output, but the process was intense.

In order to maximize the draft, I had to maintain a constant two-inch buffer from his wheel. I even tapped his wheel a few times, as I adjusted to meet his output. Trying to anticipate any sudden moves, I watched David's back wheel. We worked on clear communication, as I placed my faith in David's ability to maintain constant speed, and we fell into a routine.

David Henry was in his early forties at the time, with an undiagnosed form of ataxia. This is not uncommon. Most individuals with a genetic disease experience an odyssey during the diagnosis process. David's journey began after he was pulled over for drunk driving—although he didn't drink—and was arrested. After spending a night in jail, he was determined to find answers.

For some, the discovery of a clear answer never happens. In David's case, he never received a specific diagnosis. Based on his fundamental symptoms, he and a good neurologist figured out that he had symptoms identical to ataxia-related diseases (possibly an undiscovered version).

You have to be extremely motivated to get answers, and some-times the disease remains a mystery. It's not simple for a neurolo-gist to provide a genetic analysis. In the early days, a diagnosis involved a lot of guesswork. Even now, if a doctor orders a DNA test, the insurance company might not cover the costs.

This aspect of the unknown is a large feature of a rare disease, and perhaps it contributed to my own desire to push harder than necessary. Even then, on that roller-coaster highway, I wanted to ride beyond my means. While a shortened crank improved my situation and allowed me to depend on my one good leg, I gave into the reality. I couldn't manage the repetition. Unless I eased up, I wouldn't make it, so I rolled to a stop at the bottom of the next hill, unable to move.

My dad and uncle pulled up and jumped off their bikes.

"What's up," said Uncle Steve. "You stopping for a photo op?"

"The hill's too steep. I can't make it." I wasn't worried anymore about physically covering every inch of the ride. I was more inter-ested in making sure our team finished each day. And I was tired.

"Let's just get this done," I said. "Give me a boost."

My dad remembered the second day of the trip, when we got in the truck, with me ranting at both my parents. "You sure you want to do this?"

I wanted to move on.

Uncle Steve was eager to push ahead. He also didn't dwell too much on intimate issues. "What are you guys talking about?"

"Never mind," said my dad. "Let's keep moving."

"Onward," Uncle Steve agreed.

My dad and uncle positioned themselves on opposite sides of my recumbent, grabbed the rear rack with their free hand, while steering their bikes with the other. It was an awkward maneuver because their road bikes were taller, and they had to stoop over to reach my frame.

We were riding (now pushing) just east of Bastrop, a town near the gateway of Bastrop State Park where we had camped the previous night. I listened to their cleats click on the pavement, as they trotted up the hill. My dad's breathing was heavy from the exertion, but my uncle used another approach. He substituted hard breathing with intermittent humming, flipping through a catalogue of his favorite country songs, from Johnny Cash and Merle Haggard to Jimmy Buffett and obscure blues songs about women long gone.

David Henry rode on to meet his father, Dave, who would often drive ahead and preview the route and report on obstacles or road construction. This way we could anticipate segments of the route and pace ourselves, accordingly.

Every hill we ascended, we rode down the next, until we reached the bottom, then began the process again. Finally, we reached the top of an incline that offered a decent downhill run. David was waiting at the top.

Traversing hills always involves gear changes. Going uphill, you shift gears to make pedaling easier. Going downhill, you shift to the big chain ring in the front, which allows you to pedal harder and gain more speed. Sometimes you can hit 35 mph, especially when you're sitting so low to the ground. The wind hits your face, the ground rushes past, and everything's a blur.

After we began our descent, I looked in my rear-view mirror and David's legs were spinning like a circus clown on a bike. *Why isn't he shifting to his big chain ring?* When we reached the bottom, David told us his bike had never been adjusted to click into the big ring.

That night at dinner, Uncle Steve started calling him "Spinner." I had just met David so I didn't know how he'd react to a little ribbing. But we all laughed and I was a little jealous because who gets to have a cycling code name? The name Spinner stuck and eventually we adjusted the tension in the derailleur cable and he could keep up on the downhills.

After two days of endless hills and shoulderless roads, we stopped at a small RV park in Navasota, Texas. We circled the "wagons" as Wally fired up the barbeque. We waited for dinner and sat outside in the lawn chairs as it grew dark. My dad spread out the trip map on the grass, while we sipped our drinks, ate some cheese and crackers, and gazed at the stars.

As my dad paced around the glow of the camp lights, we discussed our route options. He stood over the map to point out some item, while I sat on the ground and announced the small print.

I watched my mom, setting up camp, preparing the corn and potato salad. I turned to my dad, his face animated as he addressed the task at hand. No doubt, my life had taken a devastating turn. I had no control of my physical situation, and I couldn't predict the future. But as I watched the hard shadows on my parents' faces, their son facing a shortened life, I understood why this was "our" disease, and why "we" have FA, and it had nothing to do with blame and everything to do with unconditional love.

CHAPTER 7

This Cure
Not for Heroes

opened my eyes and stared at the bunk above. My dad snored as my mom turned over. A few generators kicked on in the RV park north of Houston.

I swung my feet over the side of the bed and dropped unsteadily onto the cool linoleum. I pulled my *rideATAXIA* T-shirt off the counter and steadied myself on the bench, the counter, and the sink as I stumbled quietly to the bathroom.

Navigating a trailer bathroom is an Olympic moment for anybody, much less someone who lacks equilibrium. Trailers are designed for economy first, then comfort. Once you manage to squeeze through the bathroom door, your shoulders press against both walls. Then you must lift one foot to flush the commode, forcing you back against the wall.

When Wally Krill knocked on the door, he shouted with his typical enthusiasm for life.

"Good morning, everyone! It's a beautiful day!" I practically fell over. Wally's zest included positive excitement even at the crack of dawn.

I negotiated a path to our economy-sized dining table, poured a healthy serving of Raisin Bran into a paper bowl, and thought about the day.

We planned to leave the trailer, bikes, and gear at the RV park to drive into Houston. FARA had helped us arrange a meeting with some of the foremost scientists at the Albert B. Alkek Institute of Biosciences and Technology. Our host was Dr. Robert Wells, the founding director of the Biosciences Institute, and Dr. Marek Napierala.

At the time, Houston was a happening place for FA research. In the mid-1990s, several scientific teams in France, Italy, Germany, the UK, and the United States had been leveraging advances in technology and our understanding of the human genome to discover the gene responsible for Friedreich's ataxia. One of those teams included Dr. Sanjay Bidichandani, who was working in a lab at Baylor College of Medicine in Houston with Dr. Massimo Pandolfo, both of whom are among the top contributors to the FA scientific community. In 1996, Dr. Pandolfo discovered the gene mutation that causes FA.

Immediately after the gene was discovered and the findings published, Dr. Robert Wells—already an expert in triplet repeat diseases—began research on FA. He brought extensive research "capital" to the project, a man who had participated in solving the genetic code during the 1960s. His postdoctoral mentor, Dr. H. Gobind Khorana, received the Nobel Prize in 1968 for those discoveries.

In other words, I was excited. I was about to peer behind the curtain of science and meet the wizards who were exploring the workings of human life. Even more importantly, they were seeking a cure for my disease.

Dr. Wells's team was focused on the nature of molecular structures formed by the lengthy triplet repeats found in FRDA cells. Their goal was to develop therapeutic strategies and determine how to intervene at the mechanism of the disease.

But as we drove toward Houston and this scientific journey into a cure, I was thinking about Frisbee. I recalled playing Frisbee at UC Davis with a friend during a much-needed break from math homework, both of us enjoying the vast intramural green beneath a perfect blue sky. My throws were not great, but my friend ran down and caught every one. When the Frisbee returned to me and floated down directly in front of me, I missed the catch every time. Damn, I'd say, then laugh nervously.

I tried to act noble, but I hated it. I was in my early twenties, with a mind on fire and ready to make my mark. Before my disease accelerated, like any kid, I depended on my physical drive to navigate the world. I was switched on, driven and determined, and I threw myself into every activity.

Even then, I knew that I faced the paradox of my disease. While my physical impulses overcompensated any challenges, my body wasn't along for the ride. Every physical challenge was met with neurological resistance. I stumbled, fell, and missed.

With the majority of the FA population facing the disease in their youth, thousands of children navigate a similar reality. Children and teenagers live and breathe this contradiction of terms every day. While our spirits thrive and expand, our bodies give us a different message: Stop moving. Slow down. Sit.

Approaching Houston with my dad at the wheel, I stared out the window. Sure, I'd like to play Frisbee again—not just miss every throw, but catch every one. Yeah, in two years I would like to walk again. I imagined the endpoint, where Friedreich's ataxia gets resolved, and thousands of children won't have to experience the bottom of a wheelchair, a feeding tube, or the endpoint of heart failure.

I watched the sprawling metropolis come into view, a conglomeration of gray buildings, glass skyscrapers, and elevated freeways. I watched trucks pass, hauling every imaginable freight over the highway system. Overhead, planes crisscrossed the sky above the flat crescent of the Gulf. And somewhere in the middle of all this sat a research facility that could inform answers to my conundrum.

I wasn't alone in this hope. When individuals feel threatened by an outside force, people step into action. Patients and advocates are drawn into the struggle that threatens the lives of those they love.

For those performing the science, their ambitions are often underscored by the problem-solving drive of the hero. The tendency can distort the process and remove the patient from the equation. For those suffering from the collateral damage of the disease, the urgency for solutions may threaten a measured response to the discovery process.

Let's say your child has a life-threatening disease. You've learned that a therapeutic medicine has appeared on the horizon, one that will slow the advancement of the disease. The clinical trials won't resolve for another two years but that's going to create a lot of hope. You might sit back and say: Great, let's wait for that cure.

Then, one year later, the clinical trials are abandoned because they discovered an unforeseen toxic side effect. Hope is crushed. Your life (and your child's) sinks into despair.

I was the man on that roller coaster. I had the expectation that somehow this disease would get cured. I *wanted* something to happen. Perhaps even, as a result of my ride, I would make something happen. I was going to facilitate a change, a great discovery that would keep me out of the wheelchair. I could play Frisbee with my brother, get married, have kids, and live a long life.

Scientists and researchers, advocates and patients often get caught in this confusing tangle of priorities and desires. The patient clings to unrealistic hope, expecting results without understanding the true potential for success. The scientist loses sight of the patient and focuses on the cells in the dish. As a result, the disease becomes objectified, narrowed down to a problem that must be solved, the human element diminished to an abstraction.

When I arrived in Houston, I was beginning my journey as a patient advocate who helps build bridges between patients and scientists.

We pulled up to the front of the research facility, and my dad came around to help me out of the truck. I stumbled onto a Houston street, anticipating the momentous occasion. When scientists perform their work in a vacuum and the research community overlooks the patient role, the entire research progression suffers. I was there to make a difference.

I walked toward the glass doors, curious and vulnerable, unaware of how truly essential my role would become in the ensuing dialogue between patient and science for my life-threatening disease.

Mostly, I wanted to appear dignified.

The Albert B. Alkek Institute is on the outer edge of downtown Houston in the middle of the largest medical city in the world. It boasts the world's largest children's hospital, the world's largest cancer hospital, and the world's highest patient turnover. The Texas Medical Center is not just a collection of medical buildings; it's a massive city spread out across 1,345 acres, the eighth largest business district in the United States.

We had reached the Emerald City, home to the wizards of science, on the frontiers of research. The masters were standing on the other side of the massive glass doors in the lobby, awaiting our arrival.

Warm smiles greeted us. Dr. Wells treated us like visiting dignitaries. Beneath his blue eyes swirled an ocean of knowledge. His expression hinted at things I could never dream of knowing. Over his lean frame, he wore a mock turtleneck with a tan jacket and dark slacks. When he offered his hand to shake, his grip meant business.

Dr. Marek Napierala smiled. His entire body appeared to nod as he bent forward from the waist several times. He wore a crisp button-down short-sleeve shirt, shaking hands with each person like they were long lost friends. His colleague, Dr. Albino Bacolla, stood next to him, smiling and sizing up our group.

Soon, we went upstairs to a conference room, where we sat around a large wooden table. Dr. Wells talked about his research history with triplet repeat diseases, and even gave me a signed copy of his book, *Genetic Instabilities in Neurologic Diseases*. He described a notion called "sticky DNA," a concept that his team had investigated at length, where too many repeats in the DNA causes the strands to fold back on themselves.

It was a lot to absorb, but he offered a language to simplify my disease. He talked about a recent paper that detailed how Friedreich's ataxia is caused by a huge "expansion" of GAA repeats in the first intron of the frataxin gene. This expansion results in reduced production of a protein called *frataxin*. Reduced frataxin means reduced energy production in the cells of the body, which causes me to stumble down the street, grab onto walls for support, and spill my martini at a party.

The discovery of the mutation in the frataxin gene was significant. It meant genetic testing for the disease would be available. Doctors and patients didn't have to struggle through a guessing game of an often inaccurate clinical diagnosis. I have friends who sought help well before this discovery, when misdiagnosis was common. Individuals suffered for years without any sense of the cause of their body's dysfunction.

Genetic discovery also meant that the research community could begin to investigate therapeutic options, and research funding could target the cause of the disease more accurately.

Until that point, FA research was scarce and much less targeted. Imagine a boxing match where the lights are turned off and you're randomly punching in the dark. You can't find your opponent. You don't know where to direct your punches. The discovery of the gene was like flipping on the lights. Suddenly, we could see our opponent. We knew the cause of our disease. We were able to focus, and start landing blows.

When we learn the cause of a disease, we can study the mechanism. This is where research (and work toward a cure) begins.

"Then you can use basic science to look at the disease," Dr. Napierala explained in his friendly Polish accent. "When you study the basic mechanism of the disease—for example, how [DNA] *repeats* inhibit transcription, you can try to find what's wrong, what's the basis."

Discovering a cure, however, is not a straight line, he says. It's more like crossing a frontier with unknown domains.

"You have to come at incurable diseases with an open mind. You don't know what will be the cure. You can make predictions, but sometimes those questions become obsolete, and you still have to push ahead."

That's why, today, although cautious, Marek places a high value on patient/researcher relationships. When researchers collaborate with the patient community, the knowledge base accelerates the flow of vital information. The human factor increases motivation, as well, inspiring scientists to push ahead.

Before our team arrived in Houston, Marek had immersed himself in advanced genetic research, but he hadn't met anyone with FA. He pointed to a historical trend, which keeps patients and researchers apart. For example, during medical conferences, when knowledge in the field gets exchanged among scientists, the patient community is absent. The scientific community might believe they have a sound rationale for this separation.

"Let's say we have a specific cellular model we want to examine or discuss," Marek says. Perhaps these models even demonstrate promise for a therapeutic treatment. When hypothetical treatments are openly discussed in a scientific forum, vulnerable patient representative conference attendees—at least the thinking goes—might want to push untested ideas onto the research pipeline. "There's a likelihood that the patient will want to pursue research before it's fully vetted."

Urgency for a cure always complicates the dialogue between the research and the patient community. The relationship requires sensitivity.

"There have to be interactions between patients and researchers," says Marek, "but it has to be monitored. It depends upon the maturation process of both patient and scientist, where the two need to work together to move forward in the field. As the patient becomes more educated, then the ability for the two communities to work together develops."

Dialogue pushes understanding in both directions. When patients and family look at research and expect black-and-white answers, they don't exist; however, when patients can temper their reactivity, and learn how to manage their own expectations, they can maneuver around the complexity of the science. They can learn the language of the disease, and build a knowledge base that leads to understanding.

Marek believes the hard divisions between patients and researchers are starting to thaw. Scientists realize the value of placing a human face on disease and patients are learning the science.

"For scientists without the face of the disease," Marek says, "research becomes a theoretical pursuit. You read papers, study the science, and it's all in your mind, until you actually have contact with a patient."

When a patient shows up in his lab and meets other scientists, researchers, and lab technicians, the experience changes everyone's perspective.

"We're able to say: *This disease is rather different*. The patient becomes a measurable form," says Marek. The dialogue levels the playing field between patient and researcher.

After our discussion in the conference room, we toured the facility. I felt lighter, buoyed by the input of knowledge. Marek led us to a lab and pulled open a freezer kept at minus-80 degrees centigrade. The frosted drawers were filled with vials that, in all likelihood, contained a vial with *my* genetic material, since I had been donating for more than five years. This was a product of the FA Natural History Study.

When FARA was established for research funding, one strategy was to begin a *natural history study* of FA. This type of study calls upon patients not only to volunteer their genetic material but also to participate in annual physical exams, ultimately leading to the creation of a database containing the story of the progression of FA.

After I was diagnosed with FA, I would fly down to the UCLA Ataxia Clinic each year for my annual contribution. The research team, led by Dr. Susan Perlman, would collect data that would help answer specific research questions. How does FA change over time? What are the unique stages of the diseases for different people at age five, age twenty, or age forty given a certain number of triplet repeats? How do the repeats manifest in different cell types and tissues? How does the disease disrupt bodily functions and affect quality of life?

During my visits, I had to complete a series of tests, which included a range of activities—like standing on one foot, touching my finger to my nose, or making odd statements to the neurologist such as, "the president lives in the White House," and "the traffic is heavy today." Dr. Perlman would listen carefully and jot my score in a notebook.

I was a rat in the lab, but I understood its value.

When you're launching an organization focused on a treatment and a cure, a natural history study doesn't seem very sexy—it's certainly not a cure—but twenty years later this data is FARA's most valuable asset. With this data, the research community can observe how the disease changes over time. That's priceless, especially when you're able to compare the effects of a potential drug to the risk of doing nothing.

Pharmaceutical companies love this data. Companies like Horizon, Pfizer, Reata, BioMarin, and Takeda work closely with FARA because the Natural History Study provides crucial data for the initial stages of planning a drug trial. Based on the historical progression of the disease, investigators can more accurately predict how many patients will be needed and the length of the trial, in order to produce results that will be statistically significant.

Drug trials are always challenging to launch. If you want enough participants you need to organize the community, which leads to the creation of a patient registry.

Along with the Natural History Study, FARA also started building the patient registry at the beginning when it might not have

seemed like the best use of time and investment to families seeking a cure—but now it is another one of FARA's most valuable
resources. The FA patient registry is an online database where
patients can input their basic info and then when there is a clinical trial, FARA sends a notice out to all the people who fit the
inclusion/exclusion criteria and they can volunteer for the study.
Every study creates a specific framework for the inclusion criteria
of the clinical trial—age, onset of symptoms, triplet repeats. This
criterion is important to the success of the trial.

After twenty years FARA is able to provide critical information
to accelerate research, offering a pool of people who fit multiple
criteria because of the hundreds of people who have contributed
and continue to be engaged with the natural history study and
the patient registry.

Dr. Sanjay Bidichandani, part of the team that discovered
the gene responsible for FA, agrees this information is crucial.
His work as the director of the Genetics Research Laboratory at
the University of Oklahoma Health Sciences Center places him
squarely in ongoing research focused on therapies for Friedreich's
ataxia. He has received multiple grants from FARA over the years
to fund his ongoing research, and continues to have a strong relationship with the community.

Several times a year, patients and their families who are interested in connecting to the scientific community visit the lab. Bidichandani says, with a productive interaction between patients
and researchers, the mutual exchange profits the community in
measurable ways.

"Families and patients start to see what goes into the research,"
he says. "On the research side, the technicians and trainees get

fired up about what they're doing. It becomes a way for us to explain the relevance of our work."

Researchers see how the disease physically manifests in a person. They see the actual effects of frataxin deficiency and iron overload in cells, which translates to walking, talking, and managing the physical realm. Some of these observations might lead to insights, creating more questions and more opportunities.

"When we were working on the discovery [of the gene]," recalls Bidichandani, "we were working with tubes of DNA."

Those tubes of DNA come from somewhere, and that's the patient community. As soon as patients step into the process, the science accelerates. "We wouldn't be able to accomplish our work without the hundreds of donations from the patient community," Bidichandani says.

Now the voices of patient advocacy groups have been audible for several decades, and the volume is reaching a critical mass.

"The patient voice, in the case of FA and others, has now been heard by the regulatory guys and people in academia," says Bidichandani. "The patient has matured as a collaborative member of the endeavor to work on this condition."

Most importantly, children and teenagers have emerged as a vital part of this process. Bidichandani says the research community is finally hearing from young patients who are facing the disease at a crucial point in their development. "Older people talk about insurance," he says. "Younger people talk about their experience."

With younger patients, you get more honesty. You get a window of vulnerability that communicates the subtlety of the experience.

"When you meet a fourteen-year-old who's had FA for a year or two, their vocabulary is such a rich source of information," says Bidichandani.

Even now, ten years later, the research industry extends a hesitant hand to the patient community but objectifying the patient is not anyone's fault. This disposition is built into the system.

Consider a pharma company that has 80,000 employees and hundreds of offices all over the world. I've interacted with incredibly genuine people at huge pharma companies, but the person-to-person context gets lost when a nebulous bureaucracy becomes attached to the process. The patient becomes a statistic, a selling point, and an aspect of the company's profitability and growth prospects. In this scenario, the system is inherently dangerous to the patient. This circumstance reflects in the patient view of the industry, and the cycle of mistrust continues.

Walking through this research facility, however, my skepticism was beginning to diminish.

Before I visited the facility in Houston, I was afraid the research team was going to sell me the equivalent of snake oil—a vision of a cure that I desperately wanted. I had already participated in studies and put hope in treatments that didn't work.

As I witnessed physical progress in the research lab, accomplished by real people, I felt a sense of elation. I realized how my suspicions evolved from an ignorance of the science, as well as a limited understanding of the people working behind the scenes. I saw serious work happening by researchers who had committed their lives to discovery.

The more I learned about the science, the more I understood how *I* could impact progress. Perhaps I don't know what to look for through the lens of a microscope, but I can raise the money for someone who does. I can promote excitement in the FA community to encourage faster movement. I can volunteer for research studies. I can participate in outreach that connects others who are lost in the desolation of the disease.

Perhaps I am a statistic, a measurable input for the research community, but it's my responsibility to become a statistic that acts, one that inserts itself into the process, until it becomes an essential ingredient.

Until it becomes a "me."

When we understand the complexity of our disease, we can affect the reality of our choices. We can live lives in the present tense, rather than operating on assumption or a vague sense of hope. We can actively redefine our roles within the framework of the community.

After the tour of the facility, Bob Wells took our team out to dinner at a Mexican restaurant where I ate the best enchilada of my life. The experience reinforced a productive relationship that continues to this day. Though Dr. Bob Wells has retired, Dr. Napierala continues to be a strong contributor to the FA scientific community with a lab of his own solely dedicated to FA research.

THE LAST FEW MILES OF TEXAS

We left the RV park in Conroe the next day. We were joined by Angela Cloud, who had also toured the research facility with us. Her husband has a type of ataxia called spinocerebellar ataxia type 1 (SCA1), which affects many members of his family—two of his siblings, as well as four nieces and nephews. The symptoms are similar to FA, but the onset typically occurs later in life. A different gene causes SCA1 as well as a different trinucleotide repeat (CAG). The onset of SCA1 usually occurs in adulthood, which at least allows children to have a childhood. I lived the first seventeen years of my life without knowing about FA. If I could have prolonged my experience, I would have.

But disease catches up to everyone, no matter what type.

Angela supported her husband by volunteering as a leader in the Houston area for the National Ataxia Foundation (NAF). She rode with our team for about twelve miles before she had to take off but she made a difference. When people entered and exited our experience, a larger perspective began to form.

That perspective translated to purpose, and we pushed ahead. The hills rolled on for miles, even days, until we transitioned to the flat bayou land on the lower gulf. Marshes led to green pastures, and herds of cattle, water birds filled the skies, and the terrain was underscored by a tropical density that clung to the bald cypress and pine, carpeting the entire region in a wet, humid cloud. We rolled past a few farms, which appeared dry and undeveloped, perhaps as a result of the poor limestone and granite soil that lies beneath the Gulf.

After we left the Houston research facility, my pedal strokes changed. For the first time in my short riding career, I experienced the distinction between pedaling *hard* and pedaling *strong*.

Cycling toward the Louisiana border, I began to pedal strong.

When you pedal "hard," there's less purpose. You pedal with unrestrained and unfocused energy. With *hard*, there's effort but without the temperance of control. The previous year, when I attempted to ride from Sacramento to San Francisco, I was a novice rider. I was driven to succeed, focused on overcoming the challenge, and I pedaled hard. As a result, I injured my knee, which now impacted the entire ride across the country.

When you pedal "strong," you exert more control in your riding. You have more purpose, more awareness in each revolution of your cranks. The experience translates to less effort. Your posture changes, your breathing changes, and, most important, you don't wear yourself out.

It doesn't hurt to know *what* you're riding for.

We rode seventy miles that day, pedals spinning, our legs burning, with the anticipation of the Louisiana border a few miles away. We had spent twenty-eight days in Texas, which would end up being more than half our entire trip. When we hit Route 190, passing through the small logging town of Bon Weir, I could taste the humidity rising on both sides of the Sabine River—marking the boundary of the Louisiana/Texas border.

With hours of pedaling to reflect on my life, I remembered a visit to my college newspaper several years earlier. I wanted to drop off a flyer about International Ataxia Awareness Day. I walked down the stairs and stumbled into the basement, holding onto the rail. I was trembling, my heart pounding because I was going to talk to a stranger about FA, a reality of my life that I preferred to obscure. I walked up to the window and mumbled something about "national awareness day" but I failed to say ataxia.

"Oh cool," the guy said. "But what awareness day?"

I threw down the flyer and stumbled away as quickly as I could.

At that point, I was still ashamed of my disease. In my mind, shedding light on this unknown disease wasn't newsworthy. But mostly, I was promoting something that threatened my life, with little knowledge about the disease, the science, even my potential to live a full life.

I didn't feel hope.

Now, as I was about to reach another American state, that frame of mind continued to shift. I resolved to treat myself better, and to accept that when I learn one thing, there are five more questions, with twenty more potential answers—and that's okay. I understood that finding the cure is not about the immediacy of today, but about the process of *reaching* tomorrow. Change can happen...with time.

As Drew Dudley, an amazing speaker and thinker, said, "There is no world. There's only six billion understandings of it." If we create a positive image of disease and disability, then having a disease becomes about what we *can* do, not what we *can't*.

The ride had become larger than fulfilling my own needs. I was stepping out of my shell, witnessing my emergence into a collective identity.

A TEXAS MAP BURNS

After we crossed the Texas border, we spent the night at an RV campground in Louisiana. We were relieved to bid farewell to Texas and we had a Texas map-burning ceremony at the campsite that night.

Spinner and his father, Dave, Wally, Mary, Uncle Steve, and my Mom all stood in a circle around the fire. My dad held our Texas map above the ground and said a few ceremonial words. "Texas, thank you for the decent weather and the fond memories. It was fun while it lasted, but it's time to move on. Good riddance."

He lit the corner of the map with a barbecue lighter. The paper exploded into flame before fluttering to the ground. The flames lit up our faces as everyone cheered, clapped, and high-fived. Another state down, and one more step toward the finish line.

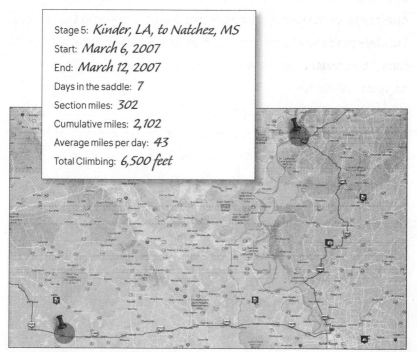

Stage 5: *Kinder, LA, to Natchez, MS*

Start: *March 6, 2007*

End: *March 12, 2007*

Days in the saddle: *7*

Section miles: *302*

Cumulative miles: *2,102*

Average miles per day: *43*

Total Climbing: *6,500 feet*

Map data ©2018 Google via ridewithgps.com.

CHAPTER 8

Change Sounds Good in Theory

*L*ouisiana summoned our team across a different planet. This new planet was covered in water.

Growing up in California, I understood the West. I understood dry desert, rocks and lizards. I understood brown grass and drought tolerant trees and the Sierra Nevada foothills, where oak, pine, and native scrub carpeted the valleys.

As we transitioned into the Deep South, those familiar signposts disappeared. Instead, all organic substance perspired and dripped in the tropical humidity that soaked the terrain. Alligators dove beneath flat bottom boats. Thick vines dangled from trees in a curtain of green, creeping across the landscape.

Earlier that morning, we said goodbye to Dave and Spinner at our campground near the border, where our Texas maps smoldered beneath a Louisiana sky. We shot down Highway 190 toward Baton Rouge like three bullet trains—Uncle Steve, my dad, and me.

For fifty miles, at a mere sixteen feet above sea level, we rode on an elevated highway built on three feet of gravel over an endless swamp. During the next few days we pushed "strong," passing patchworks of farmland, leafy trees, and the occasional field.

This was a watery world. With the slightest nudge from Mother Nature, a sea of water could submerge the entire Gulf region, as Hurricane Katrina violently demonstrated a year and a half earlier.

On both sides of the road, pear-shaped trees lifted out of the water, exposing enormous root systems that gripped the mud. Moss hung from branches where thousands of birds dipped and perched over the murky bayou. The sound of frogs, crickets, and water animals exploded in every direction. When trees thinned, giant lily pads appeared in the clearings where water rats foraged for food among the matted root systems.

Nutria rats—as they're commonly called—aren't exactly rats. They're bigger than a groundhog and smaller than a beaver, and are part of the Rodentia family, like squirrels, beavers, guinea pigs, rats, and mice. Whenever a marsh appeared, we'd see them swimming along the surface of the water, slipping beneath the giant lily pads, and then coming up for air.

These rat creatures—more closely related to porcupines or the South American capybaras—are an invasive species. They decimate swampland by feeding on the base of plant stems and roots, turning grassy marshland into barren open water in a few short years.

With nutria rats tipping the balance of a healthy ecosystem, the State of Louisiana instituted an eradication program by creating an open season on nutria, offering five dollars for every dead rat in a sack.

We'd see them on the side of the road, smashed by the grill of a speeding truck or sedan. We had encountered plenty of roadkill, but Highway 190 won the award for most roadkill—dogs, cats, snakes, frogs, turtles, rabbits, armadillos, opossums, hawks, a coyote, and a bobcat. I lost count but armadillos probably won the award for most-pasted-dead-animal on the highway. I've never actually seen a live armadillo but there are probably a few near Highway 190 in Louisiana.

We pushed across smooth, black asphalt with temperate weather and the winter sun at our backs. The unobstructed highway steered us down a path toward the Mississippi River, leading us to New Orleans and the laboratory of Dr. Ed Grabczyk. Grabczyk's project at the time was an example of lab work approached from a design perspective. He worked to construct a cell that behaves like a cell affected by Friedreich's ataxia, then he applied different compounds to study the outcome.

As we neared our final research facility, I considered a feeling that had nagged me since we left Texas. FA had forced me to reconfigure the story that I had told myself for many years. I was leaving the go-it-alone existence, the myth of the American Dream, where, with a sharp tug on the bootstraps, you could lift yourself out of a compromising situation.

If I were to thrive in my life ahead, I would have to fully commit to a collaborative existence. It sounded positive and noble, but I wasn't entirely sure about this new framework.

I still didn't want FA to be my defining feature. I had things to *prove* to the world. How could I accomplish those goals as a man identified by disease? How could I commit to a community that identified its members by the disease they shared?

I knew the wheelchair was getting closer every day, and that there was no way around being "a man with a disability." But as this conception started to fully seep into my life, I grew more tormented. I was twenty-five. My self-image depended on what others thought of me. I wanted to be functional, capable, and independent. This worldview mirrored my values.

But as I struggled with this worldview, and the inevitability of my disease, a new value system moved forth. Until that point in my life, as long as I ignored my disease, I didn't have to take responsibility. I could pretend that I was an able-bodied young man. I could downplay my lurching, weaving, and stumbling self.

Over the next week, this trip would throw these complexities in my face with the arrival of an additional rider.

As we neared Baton Rouge, we passed fields filled with water and reeds rising out of the swamp. Crawfish traps were spaced out along the top of the water, with men lingering in their flat bottom boats, harvesting their crop. Birds darted overhead, clouds of wings forming circles, then parting to regroup above another patch of water.

We stopped at a roadside café where it appeared we were the only customers for the entire day. My uncle ordered the crawfish etouffee and my dad and I ate catfish sandwiches—fillets of catfish fried in thick batter served on sliced sourdough with vinegar, the endurance snack of the South.

Supercharged from our gourmet lunch, we pushed ahead

across the flat terrain, then stopped dead. We faced a causeway, two lanes in each direction, a three-inch shoulder (meaning *no* shoulder) bordered by a concrete barrier. In other words, easy for a motorist to barrel over us without a thought.

We discussed calling for the SAG wagon to rescue us but decided to risk becoming roadkill. We even saw a few furry humps along the causeway.

My dad shrugged and clipped in. "Let's go," he said as he folded up his rearview mirror. "If it's my time, I don't want to see it coming."

We cranked at maximum effort in the middle of the slow lane for what felt like five miles with cars and trucks passing us at 65 mph to the left. It was like riding down a hallway. With the sun bouncing off the bright concrete, our wheels spun across a long stretch of what looked like white paper. My legs burned. Dad wanted to throw up. My uncle was standing over his saddle. Our speed didn't really matter, but it made us feel like we were doing something. After twenty minutes of all-out riding, we reached the other side.

As we neared Baton Rouge, the evidence from Hurricane Katrina was everywhere. New Orleans to the south got the biggest headline—80 percent of the city was flooded—but Baton Rouge was equally affected. We rode past cars buried beneath layers of dirt and mud, stilt houses rising above the chaos, where other buildings and houses were partially buried. Reconstruction efforts were in process, and machinery moved wreckage and mud, dirt and lumber, cement and steel across the highway. I felt the emotional intensity, even after a year and half.

We've all seen the effects of natural disasters from the safe distance of our televisions or newspapers and computers, but as the debris from the hurricane came into view, I grew overwhelmed with 360-degrees of reality. More than 1,200 people died in the flooding, and after witnessing the devastation, I understood.

We rode through Baton Rouge wanting to turn north and keep riding, but we had arranged to tour part of the Louisiana State University's Department of Genetics in New Orleans.

Dr. Ed Grabczyk, a Harvard-educated scientist, led a team focused on developing therapies for degenerative conditions associated with aging. In order to understand neurodegenerative diseases and the pathologic conditions related to aging, Dr. Grabczyk's attention had turned to Friedreich's ataxia, specifically the GAA repeat expansion.

GAA expansion contributes to the main cause of reduced frataxin. Since frataxin is a protein that plays a key role in energy production in the mitochondria, mitochondrial dysfunction results when there's not enough frataxin.

Researchers like Grabczyk want to understand the causes of this expansion, with the goal of determining how expansion impairs gene expression in FA. This kind of curiosity intrigued me at the Grabczyk lab.

As the scientific community builds an understanding of cause, therapeutic treatments can prevail and eventually suggest a path to a cure. After Houston, I understood that with the right questions, we could move to the front lines of this disease.

Ask the right questions, and you can retrieve your power. You can form your own opinions and figure out how to move ahead. That's when I began to feel in control again. I was learning how to respond to my disease rather than feel victimized.

We arrived at the ten-story building that housed Grabczyk's

lab. The Friedreich's Ataxia Research Alliance and the National Ataxia Foundation had arranged our team to meet with three other local families for a tour of the facility. Several people sat in wheelchairs in front of the building. I was struck by the familiar scene. Wheelchair-bound individuals facing a life sentence with the grace of a saint.

I scanned the wall of the building where I could see the water line six feet above the ground, where the flood had remained for weeks, consuming lives, and families, and loved ones. We walked into the building and the floor was completely ripped up, tarps and ladders everywhere, only one working elevator. We went around to the service elevator and rode it up to the lab.

Because of ongoing reconstruction, the lab was cluttered and disorganized. Papers, pipettes, and equipment overflowed from tables and onto the floor. I wondered how anyone could work in this environment. A team member wearing blue gloves guided a pipette to place some substance into a test tube.

Dr. Grabczyk was a soft-spoken man, tall and thin, wearing glasses perched on his nose. With tan slacks and gray sweater over a blue shirt, he seemed like a man who was as at home browsing the shelves at the local bookstore, as he was pouring over data from a genetic study.

Grabczyk lost three years of research when Hurricane Katrina cut the power to his lab. Genetic research depends on live cells that are kept in freezers at 200-degrees below freezing. No electricity. No live cells.

It's painstaking work. The cell lines are assembled by hand, then colonized in petri dishes for application in the screening process to test different compounds. Grabczyk's lab implemented high-throughput screening—an automated process that conducts thousands, even millions, of genetic and chemical tests. Some of these "screens" observe different conditions, such as an increase in frataxin production, or an improvement of mitochondrial function, or an increase in mRNA activity. These research attempts can determine if a potential compound can be developed into a therapeutic drug.

That's the big challenge, turning a compound into a patient-ready product. You can discover a compound that works perfectly in a test tube, such as increasing frataxin, but it can take years to develop a drug that is safe and effective for people.

When the hurricane hit and the power failed, the building switched over to the generators located in the basement, not on the roof. Once the basement flooded, the generators were useless. Grabczyk stored copies of cells in another facility across town, but they were destroyed, too.

Even though the lab had lost three years of work, we learned that he was still moving forward. The team knew their science was contributing to the curative process and they weren't going to let the destruction of the Gulf slow things down.

When we were on the road with just two or three riders, moving through the geography of an immense country, it was easy to feel isolated. When you include the purpose of our mission—most people we met along the way had never heard of this disease—I felt like we were moving through an insulated bubble. Standing with that group of individuals in the middle of a lab dedicated to Friedreich's ataxia research, the purpose of our ride returned. I was with people who understood the disease... understood me.

After we checked into our hotel, we walked along the Mississippi River. The water flowed black and calm, with no wind to stir the surface. City lights dimmed the stars. My dad had his arm around my mom, and we watched the barges moving down the river. Music drifted across the buildings from Bourbon Street, Cajun and jazz, and the occasional drunk person howled at the night.

We were all silent when my dad spoke.

"Kyle. Thanks for inviting me on your ride," he said.

While it might have seemed like an innocent comment, I was stunned. It was completely out of my dad's comfort zone. This from a guy who didn't want to ride for more than two weeks, from a person who's a self-professed homebody, from a man whose first thought is not *where are we going today,* but rather *the lawn needs mowing.*

RIDEATAXIA TURNS NORTH

The next morning, we returned to Baton Rouge to meet Marco Ricci, a twenty-six-year-old man with Friedreich's ataxia, and his friend Antonio Bianchi. They had flown from Italy to join us for the rest of our trip.

When I posted the idea of the cross-country ride on my blog, Marco was one of the first people to respond. He emailed that he rode a handcycle and competed throughout Europe. His goal—he claimed—was to become the best handcyclist in the world and to set an example for all disabled people. The previous year, he founded a non-profit sports association to promote sports therapy for people with disabilities.

I was excited to have him join us. Like me, he was driven to keep this disease from limiting his potential, and he wanted to be a living example of what's possible.

At first, those characteristics seemed cool and noble, even heroic. But when I looked closer, they were qualities I wanted to move past—qualities that no longer fit the purpose of this ride.

Six months before, during the planning stages, the bike ride fed my ego with a heroic bent, but that motivated me less and less now. While it's developmentally appropriate to be self-centered at twenty-five, this disease had torn at my self-image. Connecting to people impacted by similar circumstances—families and friends, children, mothers, grandparents, an uncle or a brother, entire networks of family systems grappling with disease—had changed my perspective.

Our visit to Dr. Grabczyk's research lab affirmed that shift in my outlook. My parents felt it, too. We began to understand how we fit into the larger design. Our journey wasn't just about finding a treatment *for me*, but about how we affected others along the way; it was about how we interacted with the community; it was about taking action that lifted everyone up. This was a powerful realization and it began to validate the entire trip.

I was conscious—and a bit nervous—that Marco had not yet arrived at this consideration, so I was anxious. Then again, maybe I still wanted to be the hero and I was uncomfortable to admit it.

Within sight of our end goal, nobody wanted to sit around Baton Rouge for a day waiting for Marco's plane to land. So, we rode ahead to erase any doubt about our ability to finish the journey. Once we hit fifty miles, we planned to return in the truck to Baton Rouge.

As we rode north along Highway 61, we left behind the flat bayou land, and pushed toward the uplands of Louisiana, passing through valleys with tributaries leading to the Mississippi River, which flowed to our immediate west.

Soon we left the main highway and navigated along a series of backcountry roads that would eventually lead us away from the river for a few days and through the Homochitto National Forest until we reached Natchez, Mississippi.

Leafy oak trees and pine formed a canopy overhead, obscuring the sky. Much of the day, we spent in the cool shade. We passed a few houses set back from the road. Occasionally we'd see a driveway and imagine a house at the end. Traffic was sparse, a few pickup trucks and SUVs. When cars passed, people would wave and make eye contact.

The terrain and the density of the foliage reminded me of the remote places where I've hunted and fished with my dad, brother, and Uncle Steve. But in those situations we blended into the terrain. Here we rode colorful bikes, wore bright jerseys, and were clearly not part of the environment. We felt exposed.

At one point, just before the asphalt disappeared and the road turned to gravel, we crossed a suspension bridge that leaned to one side—rusted steel, peeling paint, weathered, and worn. We arrived at a passage where the trees opened up and farmland appeared. Something on the horizon caught my eye, and I slammed on my brakes to take a picture. My dad was immediately behind me. He crashed into my trike and fell onto the road.

My dad picked himself off the ground and we completed our mileage for the day. We drove back to Baton Rouge to collect our guests at the airport. During the drive, the thick green foliage flew past my window, revealing patches of blue sky. Thinking about what I might post in the blog for the day, I considered, again, that when we pursue physical accomplishments, applying terms like "in spite of disability" or "overcoming adversity," we are unwittingly affirming a flawed societal belief system that leaves many people feeling exposed.

When you're diagnosed with a rare disease, you step into a grey area, so I'll just say it: Sometimes I am grateful for my disease.

I am obviously conscious of the destructive nature of FA, and I realize that gratitude for a debilitating disease might not be a popular concept. This perspective goes against the standard idea that there's something fundamentally wrong with disability. But I'm driven to integrate how "disability" fits into my life, to accept myself, and to disregard those social messages.

The outcome of a potentially terminal disease is tragic, but having an incurable disease doesn't make me flawed. It's often this belief—that of the "flawed" individual—whether we lack the correct physical attributes that sets us at odds with one another...or ourselves.

RIDEATAXIA

GETS INTERNATIONAL

We met the two Italians at the airport. They greeted us with suitcases, two bikes, and a wheelchair. Lots of enthusiasm, big hugs, and big smiles all around.

We piled in the Durango and sized up our new members. The conversation was halting as our guests spoke with thick accents and asked us to repeat sentences. Both of them were dressed in bright and modern clothes. Antonio was in his early fifties with gray, curly hair. He wore shorts that sat high above the knee—perhaps too high for American taste—exposing a pair of seriously hairy legs. He smiled a lot and appeared genuinely happy.

Marco had short, dark hair and a skinny face. He was muscular and lean. When you train for cycling, it's all about achieving a balance between power and weight. His body had that great ratio needed for intense riding. Back at the airport, I watched him maneuver the wheelchair with precision.

The guy had some serious arms and pecs from training on his handcycle. Since his FA began earlier than mine, he transitioned to the wheelchair in his late teens. By the time he began riding, however, he couldn't pedal a trike with his weakened legs.

It doesn't take long to lose muscle memory. If you've had an injury or a disease that attacks your coordination (like Friedreich's ataxia), and months—or even years—pass, making a transition to a seated trike can be difficult.

Imagine this. You've spent several years in a wheelchair. One morning, you wake up and say, *I'm gonna go out and buy a trike. My legs still work. My heart still pumps. Let's do it.*

But the big day arrives for your test-ride…and your knees flop inward and knock painfully together. Or they flop outward, rubbing on the tires on either side of your legs. You've lost control of your legs and it seems like the more you try, the more they flop. You need leverage and propulsion, and it's not there.

This makes a handcycle the obvious choice for people who have lost function in their legs, but it's not an easy alternative.

A few days into our ride, during a break at a historical overlook along the Natchez Trace, I sat down on Marco's handcycle—a Quickie Shark—and rode it around the parking lot for a few minutes. The experience gave me some perspective.

Handcycles require intense upper body strength—biceps, shoulders, forearm muscles—plus the concentration required to simultaneously steer, brake, and shift. I could keep the trike moving in a straight line, but I struggled to make simple turns in a circle.

The positioning is not so different from a recumbent. You're still sitting in a reclined chair, but the crank is immediately in front of your chest. Sitting down requires a little strategy. It's more like getting *in* than getting *on* because you must situate yourself between the crank and the seat.

Then there are the precise adjustments—the length of the footrest, the angle of the seat back, the length/position of the crank relative to your torso, how much your arms bend when you're completing a pedal stroke. Each adjustment affects the other, which affects your power output and how quickly you fatigue.

If something's off, your ride suffers.

After I circled around the parking lot, pedaling with my arms, I realized a simple fact: If I had ridden all day, I would be in serious pain.

With that in mind, I felt enormous respect for Marco. Here's a man, who, against his physical intuition, had squared up against his predicament and made every effort to prevail.

When we returned from the airport, it was time for dinner. My mom had prepared an Italian meal: Pasta with a jar of Ragu. An inauthentic Italian meal slightly embarrassed me, but I was even more uncomfortable explaining to Marco that we had pushed ahead earlier that day.

It was our first disagreement.

Marco told me before he joined the ride that he intended to ride every mile, so he was caught off-guard.

"Wait a minute," he said. "You've already cut off thirty miles of my ride?"

I knew this reaction was coming, and I felt defensive, so instead of trying to acknowledge his frustration, I responded with my own frustration.

"Marco, we still have four hundred miles to go," I told him, "and we had to knock off a few more miles to reach Memphis on time."

"That's not what we talked about," he grumbled, visibly annoyed. In our initial exchanges, he had asked me about all the details, our beginning point, the distances we would cover. Now, I had already shortened his distance.

I realized we were strangers, except for our emails. When we rode north earlier that day, I had made an assumption without considering his reaction. Our first interaction had placed us at odds—if only mildly—and I felt uneasy.

The next morning, we picked up Marco and Antonio drove across the Louisiana border to Centerville, Mississippi, where we'd stopped the previous day.

We dropped our bikes on the small, two-lane highway that led north through southern Mississippi. We were in an area of the state that owes much of its economic survival to the timber industry. For over 200 years, the region had harvested lumber from the Piney Woods, instituting reforestation by the early 1900s for long-term sustainable forestry.

For our purposes, this history only meant one thing: lots of logging trucks—eighteen-wheelers hauling stacks of fresh-cut trees. More big trucks with big men behind big wheels. Trucks with long beds, short beds, and guns mounted in the rear window. (Mississippi legally permits the open carrying of a long gun in a car without a permit or license.) Trucks with dogs in the passenger seat, tongues flapping in the wind.

We were about to embark for the day with a convention of trucks bearing down on us, and they paid little attention to our entourage skirting along a narrow and shoulder-free road.

Low hills, curves, obstructed views, and blind turns made everyone nervous.

Since we had more (and new) riders, we discussed our riding strategy before taking off. We explained to Marco and Antonio the importance of hugging the shoulder, and when a rider sees a car in the mirror to yell, "Car back." That alerts everyone in the group to move over to the side of the road, both for courtesy and safety. We agreed this would be our protocol.

I rode in the front. My uncle was behind me, then Marco and Antonio. Finally, my dad brought up the rear, in part, because he felt responsible for the two visitors and their safety.

Except it almost killed him.

Not long after we started off, I glanced back at Marco, who was riding down the middle of the road. He looked like he was having the time of his life. He had discovered American roads, smooth and wide. I imagined roads in Europe to be smaller, bumpier—cobblestoned even—and crowded with cars.

We were riding through a forested state in a thinly populated region, with traffic that was also sparse...until it wasn't.

That's when someone yelled, "Car back," and Marco ignored it. No reaction. No acknowledgment of the warning whatsoever. Then everyone joined in as a chorus, "Car back!" He appeared so absorbed in his momentum, head down, pushing forward, that our words floated past him.

Eventually, he scooted to the side. As soon as the truck passed, he retook his position in the middle of the road. This happened repeatedly and Marco's governing attitude became clear. You need to avoid me. Make a hole and make it wide.

We also couldn't ignore how much our pacing had slowed.

Dad, Uncle Steve, and I had been riding together for almost 2,000 miles. We understood what speed we could ride in different situations. Since the road was moderate with a few hills, we could easily maintain an average speed of 12 to 14 mph. Marco was moving much slower, between 6 and 8 mph.

We would ride ahead to a pull off. Wait. They would catch up. We would pedal ahead. Repeat. It was affecting our momentum, forcing us to adjust our time frame for the rest of the ride.

On the one hand, I was annoyed. Marco had given me the impression he was a world-class cyclist. We had talked about average speed on different terrain before he got here.

On the other, I felt guilty. These guys just landed the previous day from Italy, and we expected them to match our pacing for a fifty-mile day. They should have been resting.

After six weeks on the road, we weren't prepared to adjust our pacing. Partly, we were proud of what we had just accomplished and we didn't want it to slip away. Yes, it was selfish, but nobody wanted to spend the next 400 miles looking in the rearview mirror. We never considered that Marco wasn't ready.

Marco's idea of speed was very different. Within the first hour, I saw that he was struggling, but he chose not to show it —and I chose to ignore it.

After about an hour of shouting at Marco to keep to the side of the road—Antonio had been yelling stern warnings in Italian —we stopped to eat a granola bar. I couldn't contain myself.

"Hey, dude. Don't you hear us? We don't want anyone to die out here. You have to move over when we call car back."

"When I ride on the side of the road, my wheels get squirrely," Marco said.

We decided that my uncle and I would ride ahead to complete the miles for the day, and my dad would remain behind.

By the time Uncle Steve and I arrived at camp, the sky had grown dark. It started to rain. We figured they must be an hour behind, so we returned with the trailer to pick everyone up.

When we found them, Marco could barely sit upright in his handcycle. He was riding at about 3 mph, his body tilted over to one side. FA is an energy deprivation disease and one of the symptoms is fatigue. Put that together with forty miles on a handcycle after arriving from Italy and forget about trunk stability, but somehow, to Marco's credit, he would not stop his arms from pedaling.

My dad looked like he might strangle someone. They had so many close calls that day that he couldn't even talk about it.

"It's raining. It's dark," I said to Marco. "Let's call it a day."

Marco could barely talk. "No. I'm going to finish the ride."

We stopped in front of him and argued for a bit. The rain soaked the ground and the canopy of branches shook in the wind. We knew there were six hilly miles left, with a steady climb up to the campground. Marco was not going to make it unless we pulled him with the truck.

I got it. I've been there. You want to push ahead but you can't. Marco had his heart set on riding every single mile, but he relented. Since he was in no condition to get in the car, we pulled down the back of the trailer and pushed him in.

That night, after everyone had recovered, my dad and I met Antonio and Marco at Pizza Hut in a nearby town. Wally had encouraged me to speak with them about our vision for the ride. I was already nervous about how the rest of the trip might evolve, and I had to step forward and represent all the stakeholders in the trip.

After I ordered a Supreme Pizza—onions, mushrooms, sausage, and pepperoni—I launched into my speech.

"This ride is not about you," I told Marco. "It's not about me. It's about the FA community. We've come more than 2,000 miles, and we can't self-destruct at this last stage. We have hundreds of people cheering for our success. We all need to work together like a team."

That moment was a turning point for me, a coming-of-age. I couldn't have articulated these feelings at the beginning of the ride. Six weeks earlier, my motivation was more self-centered.

Now that center had expanded to include a vision, a greater purpose, and a community.

Marco stared down at the table. I imagine he felt embarrassed. Maybe he had heard this speech before. In fact, I felt like one of my middle-school coaches. *Think of your team. Put your ego aside. We're in this together.*

The next day, we started at the Natchez Trace, and we had one excellent day of riding. Then everything fell apart.

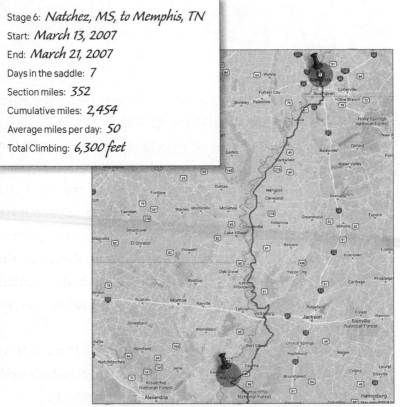

Stage 6: *Natchez, MS, to Memphis, TN*
Start: *March 13, 2007*
End: *March 21, 2007*
Days in the saddle: *7*
Section miles: *352*
Cumulative miles: *2,454*
Average miles per day: *50*
Total Climbing: *6,300 feet*

Map data ©2018 Google via ridewithgps.com.

CHAPTER 9

Finding Graceland

O ne should take an athletic adventure with a modicum of reverence. At least during work hours.

A "workday" on a cross-country bike trip begins when you clip into your pedals. You're focused on comfort, stability, mirror check, helmet, gloves, and then you hit the road. From that point forward, you've got road hazards, the intensity of your physical output, the elements—wind, rain, sun, roadkill (at this point in our trip, we could almost count roadkill as a natural element)—the collaboration of your teammates, and the focus required to succeed.

The quality of your attention translates to two items: survival and getting there.

That's why we weren't amused when we found Marco sitting on his trike outside a country store in the middle of rural Mississippi working on his second beer at nine in the morning.

We were north of the Natchez Trace, a historic migration route used by Native Americans for hundreds of years. The trail, which ran near the road in places, offered a glimpse into another time, connecting past to present as we hugged the preserved path through the leafy green.

The route had been so heavily traveled—by horses, carts, feet, families—that over several centuries, the soil had settled five to ten feet lower than the surrounding terrain.

As we rode through the thick canopy along the Trace, passing heavily wooded areas that gave way to lush green meadows, and back to forest, I imagined people walking on the path, the wind, leaves, the light falling through the trees, carrying the voices of men and women who traveled along its course.

I imagined the thousands who migrated north toward greener pastures as we pushed ahead, mirroring a similar sentiment, with the exception that we wore Spandex and rode $2,000 machines while we ate granola bars and barbecued chicken from a propane stove.

Our spirits had lifted with the ease of the ride and a trouble-free day. Since the Trace contained almost no traffic, we all decided to ride down the middle of the road in honor of our guest, who remained glued to the double-yellow line.

That night the Italians pitched a tent outside the trailer and we stayed at the Rocky Springs Campground just off the Trace. The evening included several glasses of wine and we tried to explain the meaning of the most ambiguous term in the English language—"stuff."

We woke with the morning sun breaking through the trees. We stowed our gear and got ready for the day ahead. I felt optimistic. Perhaps we could sustain our momentum with our new team members and complete the ride.

Perhaps we could absorb the complexity that new relationships bring—a bit of surrender, concessions, and the willingness to place differences aside.

Then, almost immediately after leaving the parking lot, I got a flat. Since Marco and Antonio had agreed to pedal at their own pace, they decided to push ahead. Antonio had figured out how to give Marco a boost (when needed) by pushing his front tire into Marco's rear horizontal stabilizer bar. This solution resulted in a bumping, coasting rhythm. It wasn't ideal, but they went slightly faster.

The two Italians set off and we stayed behind to fix the thirty-fourth flat tire of the trip. They weren't confident about the route so when they reached a crossroads, they decided to wait for us outside a country store. The junction contained a total of four buildings, faded wooden siding, peeling paint, and shingles falling to the ground. All the structures appeared unoccupied or abandoned. Beyond the intersection stretched miles of uninterrupted woodlands, rivers, and creeks.

Marco felt restless, impatient. He asked Antonio to step inside and buy him several beers. Understanding the stakes of the day, Antonio refused. So, Marco sat on his trike at the bottom of the wooden stairs and shouted into the market with his thick Italian accent. "Hey, can you sell me a few beers?"

When we rode up, with the morning sun shining on the country setting, Marco was just finishing his second beer. He offered us a lazy wave and a loopy smile, like we'd all be amused with his refreshment break.

We weren't. Antonio stood off to one side almost as if he didn't know the guy.

"Marco! What the hell are you doing?" I yelled. "Let's go."

Antonio looked both embarrassed and disappointed. Marco took a last slug of his beer, dropped his bottles in the dirt, and repositioned himself on his handcycle. "Let's go then," he said with a shrug. Antonio walked over and retrieved the bottles and threw them in the trash.

We continued on. Soon, we met a fast downhill that stretched through the wooded terrain. Leafy trees covered the road, and we picked up speed through a tunnel of green where daylight vanished and a muted haze reached through the canopy. We veered around potholes, branches, and brush. I had to ride my brakes just to maintain control.

I heard the beginnings of a war cry; then Marco screamed past at 40 mph. Imagine a drunk driver on a speeding handcycle on a rural country road with a mad grin on his face.

That was Marco, who ripped past me, his arms spinning, his head tilted back in ecstasy. With all the effort that a rider places into a handcycle, any downhill turns into a welcome relief, and Marco was taking full advantage of gravity.

Soon, the canopy of trees disappeared and revealed a vast green meadow where thick grass touched a distant tree line. Narrow clouds hung overhead, and a crisp breeze shook branches and tossed leaves along the ground.

The road flattened out at the bottom, transitioning into a sharp curve, and we all adjusted our speed accordingly. But Marco was out of sync with the rest of the team. He sped far ahead and failed to pick up on our collective cue. We watched him approach the curve well beyond a safe speed limit. Turning corners on a handcycle requires the rider to lean into the curve, a motion that demands aggressive trunk stability and balance. With FA, you're already compromised in both these regards, so when Marco hit the curve, we all cringed as inertia kept him moving in one direction, while the course of the road proceeded in another. He disappeared into a cloud of dust, flipping his handcycle into a barbed wire fence, just beyond a drainage ditch.

When we pulled up behind, he was pinned to the ground beneath his rig. He looked up at us, still strapped into his bike.

"See," he grumbled. "That's what happens when I get too close to the shoulder."

Marco wasn't hurt, but we were all thinking the same thing: Let's hope his bike is ruined.

Antonio situated Marco on the side of the road and inspected the bike. His patience had worn thin.

Antonio stepped over to address us out of earshot. "The bike is okay," he told us. "The man is not."

We had logged only ten miles into a fifty-mile day. His friend had already gotten drunk and flipped his bike.

"You guys go ahead," Antonio said. "I'm going to figure out what to do."

So, we pushed ahead. We had lost tolerance for our guest, and now we set our sights on Memphis. We finished the day, arriving at the campground outside Vicksburg, Mississippi, where, some say, after a forty-seven-day siege, the Civil War hit a turning point.

This was our turning point, too.

That night, my dad spoke with Antonio outside the motel where the Italians were staying. Antonio confessed he was "done." He'd decided to return to Italy the next morning.

After some discussion, we all arrived at a similar decision. It was time to part ways with Marco.

In the morning, we met with Marco in the motel dining room. We told him we couldn't finish the trip with him. Instead, we offered to put him on a bus to Memphis. Antonio seconded the offer.

"I'm getting on a bus and taking the first plane to Italy," he told Marco. "You're coming with me."

Marco—a guy who was about to be abandoned in the middle of a foreign country, who depended upon a wheelchair to navigate, who had lost favor with his hosts—responded with hubris.

"No way," he said. "I came here to ride and accomplish my goal. I'm not giving up."

I had to admire his gumption—but the mood was pretty grim. Antonio walked off to find a bus, and we left Marco sitting alone in the breakfast nook of the hotel.

As we made our way to the front door, I looked through the window at the hotel dumpster. Antonio had built a specialized wooden and aluminum carrying case for Marco's handcycle. It was thoughtfully constructed—almost affectionately—but now it was sitting in the trash.

The next day, we rode out of Vicksburg on a frontage road. We abandoned our Adventure Cycling Association map and followed a map that Wally had found, *The Mississippi River Trail Map.*

It guided us through leafy neighborhoods with small, square homes where people sat on porches drinking iced tea, facing quiet roads—perhaps a car every ten minutes—and the immense river that flowed to our left. It carried great barges down the middle, leaving the taste of diesel on our tongues. The barges plied south toward the Louisiana gulf, freighting anything from coal and corn to soybeans, timber and trash.

North of Vicksburg, we rolled past big farms with country houses every few miles, then acres of row crops and tractors moving at their persistent crawl. And there were always the obligatory single-room churches, standing nobly at the end of dirt roads.

Uncle Steve had stopped his bike to get a snack out of his jersey pocket when an elderly woman pulled up in her Datsun pickup truck. She was in her mid-eighties and wanted to hear our story, but mostly, she wanted to talk. She explained that her husband had died a few years earlier. After a while, she was silent and stared across the road to the distances beyond.

"You know," she said, "I've had a good ol' life."

It seemed like such a mundane statement, perhaps overly sentimental, but it hit me hard. I was struggling with guilt about the outcome of the past few days. I didn't want to be the cause of someone else's suffering.

I started the ride with the notion that I needed to figure out something for myself. Marco came to America with that same notion. Our lives had intersected at different points on that journey. My notion was now following a different narrative. The ride had realigned my focus by framing my actions within the greater FA community.

There's a fine line between narcissism and altruism. Sometimes it's difficult to disentangle one from the other. Perhaps "service" begins with the greatest intentions, but it can become convoluted by individual need. The difficulty exists in learning how to navigate an acceptable balance, committing to service while placating our individual urges.

I understood Marco's ambition. Several thousand miles earlier, I got angry when we chose not to pedal part of the route because of a thin shoulder and lousy sightlines. I thought about my self-righteous behavior when my mom bought the copper tree and hid it beneath a pile of jackets. My mom defused the situation because she knew me. I remembered how I pushed beyond my limits and injured my knee on the ride from Sacramento to San Francisco.

As the disease sunk its roots deeper in my body, I wanted to do anything that would allow me to maintain ownership. I wanted to preserve control. I wanted my decisions to manifest an outcome.

But that was going to be impossible. As we neared Memphis, I examined the futility of a self-centered life. I understood that in order to find balance, I had to remove myself from that center and join a circle that was connected to many individuals.

In my interactions with Marco, I was still arriving at this perspective, but I knew my survival required a revised framework. Perhaps, with time, I could have resolved to connect with him, to consider his timing, and to support him to arrive on his own terms, but we had run out of miles.

We *had* to move on.

I was angry with Marco. I believed he was self-destructive, and his actions would infect our journey. I judged his cavalier attitude, wrestling with his demons to serve his own interests, to serve his own desires, but as I pictured him struggling to arrive in Memphis on his own steam, his wheelchair strapped to his handcycle, catching rides in pickup trucks with strangers (one night he slept in his handcycle at a fire station), he was—like all of us—a man just trying to find his way.

Later that day, as we neared the campground along the river, I received a call from the executive director of National Ataxia Foundation, Mike Parent. Police in Jackson, Mississippi, had called about a man riding a three-wheel bike through a sketchy part of the outskirts of town in the dark the night before.

The man, who had a wheelchair strapped to the back of his handcycle, wore colorful attire, spoke broken English with a heavy Italian accent, and had been asking people directions to Memphis.

That's when the police turned on their lights and escorted him through town.

WE CAN ALL CARVE A PATH
OUT OF THE CUBICLE

The night after Vicksburg, we rolled up a dirt road to a campground beside the Mississippi River. My mom set up lawn chairs outside the trailer, served cheese on a platter, had beers on ice, and grapes on a plate. She wore her apron with an embroidered image of a bike on the front.

My cell phone buzzed. It was Ron Bartek, who wanted to share good news. Two months earlier, as we prepared to leave Oceanside on our cross-country trek, Ron proposed to the NAF Board of Directors that the two organizations match funds and create a grant in honor of our ride. After negotiating the details over the course of two months, the Friedreich's Ataxia Research Alliance and the National Ataxia Foundation had decided to match the funds we raised, bringing the total to $100,000 for the first Kyle Bryant Translational Research Award.

After the call, I eased into my chair and stared at the legendary Mississippi River. I felt like I just had an airport named after me. So much for keeping my ego in check.

I stared beyond the mouth of a small port just south of Greenville, Mississippi, where barges entered and exited from a refinery next door to a rice mill. Birds dove along the shore. Green forest carpeted the distant hills. When I was a kid, my mom took us to see *Big River*, a musical about Huckleberry Finn and my introduction to the Mississippi River. Growing up in a small town in Northern California, the rest of the world was a distant place. Some people never left the county. I understood Huck Finn, his desires, and the urgency to move beyond himself.

Many people assumed this ride was impossible. I had changed that. Many saw themselves in our struggle—we were a family that got dealt a lousy hand. We simply chose to do something different.

Many of us exist in situations where we feel our power slipping away from us, and we limit ourselves by what we only *think* is possible.

The scale of the ride suggested another option.

After college, I was excited to get a job at an engineering firm in Sacramento. For a while that was my dream—get a job, make money, buy a house (and I did). Then I began dreaming beyond the walls of my cubicle.

One day, as I sat at my desk at Brown and Caldwell, an email popped up on my screen. I had been reading a book about Roz Savage, a woman who rowed a boat across the Atlantic Ocean and who has since become the first woman to row solo across three oceans. She was named Adventurer of the Year in 2010 by *National Geographic*.

She had been working in a corporate job in London. She was passionate about her job, but she wanted more. Her friends and family thought she was crazy, but she wanted her world to expand beyond the walls of her cubicle. So, she got in a boat and started rowing across the oceans of the globe.

I was inspired by her journey, so I wrote her an email. She wrote back:

Kyle, good luck with your bid for freedom from the cubicle. You go for it. I'd love to hear how it all goes for you. When I look back, I wonder why it took me so long to break free. Now I am on the other side of the decision. My life feels so right and so natural—I wonder how on earth I endured all those years in the cubicle. Fear of the unknown, I guess. But now I love the uncertainty of the unknown—it's where all the really cool stuff happens.

As we pushed into Tennessee with the help of an incredible tailwind, that alternative came into view. We were cheating time, our bikes hitting 25 mph with no effort, and I was reminded of the concept of pedaling hard and pedaling strong.

In our urgency to overcome obstacles, adversity, whatever you call it, we push harder, and while we can experience some payoff, more frequently we land farther from our goal. On the other hand, when we push "strong" in real time, without the consequence of overreach, we make ourselves available to the unknown, and, most important, we leave room for insights that may surprise us.

When we reached the outskirts of Memphis we missed a turn and got lost for several miles. Best laid plans. We passed grassy fields with cattle grazing, dirt roads leading to distant farmhouses and dusty barns set back from the road. We had minimal traffic, with the occasional passing truck occupied by men wearing cowboy hats, who would offer us a two-finger wave and a nod of the head.

As we skimmed along the edges of drainage ditches and endless strands of barbed wire, I was reminded of a feeling that had surfaced over the past few hundred miles, one that took root just before Baton Rouge.

I had become thankful for my disease.

Isaac Newton said that every action has an equal and opposite reaction. My high school physics teacher, Mr. Hughes taught me that when you're pushing on a wall, the wall pushes back. FA had become that force. It pushed against me and woke up an awareness that may have never manifested. My disease gave me something to push against, demanding that I think bigger and expect more from myself.

The concept of wanting more in life is ubiquitous. Everyone has that itch.

At one time or another, you might think, *there's got to be more.* But without a sense of what you need to push against, ambiguity can undermine ambition. Then when life, say, throws a disease at you, accompanied by a progressive disability that limits you in twenty different ways, you get stuck thinking that your ability to navigate the world has diminished.

The opposite is true.

Your license to thrive has been magnified. You have been given permission to live in the moment. You're being asked to perceive your opposing force as an opportunity—an invitation to do what you love, and do it to the fullest extent.

Living without moderation is not about acting big. Instead, you learn how to get comfortable with who you have become.

I get annoyed with the concept of *anything is possible*. If you take it literally, it's a ridiculous comment. You can't fly without getting on an airplane. You can't breathe underwater without SCUBA gear.

On the other hand, while you can accept your limitations, you must be able to travel along the edges and test your limits. That's when you begin living without moderation. Thinking big and acting on those big thoughts in small ways. With this worldview, you take the entire victim perspective off the board.

I JUST RODE MY TRIKE
TO GRACELAND

Four miles across the Tennessee border, we reached Graceland, the home and final resting place of Elvis Presley. It's also a tourist destination visited by half a million every year. That day Elvis Presley Road was filled with traffic and probably not the safest route to travel, but we were determined to say that we rode our bikes to Elvis's house.

My dad, uncle, and I stood next to our bikes in front of Graceland. I knew the following year the National Ataxia Foundation conference was scheduled for Las Vegas and I said, "Hey, next year, let's ride to Vegas."

My dad rolled his eyes. "Let's finish this ride first," he said.

Eventually, we pulled away from Graceland. The houses grew closer together, the streets bigger, and the green countryside replaced the noise of the city. As we pedaled through downtown Memphis, country music blared out of diners and coffee shops. Freight trucks downshifted, horns honked, and dogs barked.

Soon, we swung a hard left from Danny Thomas Boulevard to Exchange Avenue, then pushed up a small incline to our hotel where the conference was scheduled. We had reached the end of our ride.

We pedaled past a row of cars, and I saw a crowd of people ahead. They stood at the curb and looked down the street. We heard cheers and whistling as we approached the crowd, framed by a welcome banner and balloons. Someone popped a bottle of champagne. I waved at my brother and my soon-to-be sister-in-law, who stood near Arnie Gruetzmacher, the chairman of NAF's board, and executive director Mike Parent.

With the cheers, backslapping, and high-fives, I sat in my recumbent and tugged on my beard. I was elated, but I wasn't thinking that I just completed a 2,500-mile ride. I wasn't registering the congratulations and shouts of approval from the onlookers. I wasn't even thinking I could eat two plates of enchiladas, a burrito, a slice of pizza, and a hamburger.

I was thinking about a haircut and a shave.

The appeal of the ride had been simple: All we had to do was ride our bikes. We didn't have to look nice, impress anyone, or wear a tie. At some point, we all agreed that we wouldn't shave our beards until we got to Memphis.

Now, it was time to lose the beard.

I was going to appear the next day on *The Morning Show* in Memphis so, after we checked into our hotel, I slipped away. A shoeshine man pointed me to the Down to Earth Barber.

I felt liberated, heading out on my own. I hopped on a tourist trolley—one of those local transports designed to *look* like a trolley. The sun was shining with a warm breeze blowing through the open windows. I rode through the streets, passing buildings and pedestrians. I was bursting with pride. I wanted to shout it out to everyone, "Hey, I just rode my bike here!" But the secret was mine, and perhaps that lingering feeling meant more than the actual bike ride. It was a reminder of the secret I carry every day.

Many people with a rare disease feel invisible. This knowledge consumes us. We all have the desire to be understood, to be witnessed, to be seen, and that's exactly what we need to do. We need to reach out to others, connect with community and become a part of something larger than ourselves. When you have a rare disease, stepping into community validates your existence.

Everyone says, "We need to raise awareness" but "raising awareness" typically places focus on a deficit. I don't want to raise awareness in order to focus on disease, but rather to increase the reach of our community and connect to others who feel alone and isolated.

I sat by the window of the trolley on a smooth wooden seat, my hand clasping the pole. I wore several bracelets on my wrist, each indicating various ataxia organizations, including NAF and FARA. A woman in a neighboring seat stared at me. Seeing I was unsteady on my feet, she asked about my blue bracelet, which suggested I was attending the NAF conference.

"Hey," she asked. "Are you going to see Kyle speak today?"

I stuck out my hand to her and smiled. "I'm Kyle."

She laughed, slightly embarrassed, shook my hand, and introduced me to her twelve-year-old daughter, who had a type of ataxia.

"We've been reading your blog every day," she said, "and we really admire what you've done for our community."

When the trolley dropped me down the street, I walked (well, stumbled really) into the barbershop with my head held high. Four barber chairs sat in a row. One guy was getting a haircut, another reading a paper. I tried to act cool because, as always, I saw the question marks on their faces. They're thinking, *This guy looks drunk.*

"I'm just looking for a shave," I said. "I've been on the road for three months riding my trike."

"What?" the barber said. "That's crazy. Tell me all about it."

And I did.

CHAPTER 10

The Journey Continues

Ayear later, I realized that I rode nearly across the United States and into my life's work. In 2009, when I left Brown and Caldwell, moved across the country and joined the staff of the Friedreich's Ataxia Research Alliance, we began to build a program of annual, single-day rideATAXIA events in which anyone can get involved. We now have six locations and attract over 2,500 individuals annually. Our goal—aside from advancing research through fundraising and community building—was to draw individuals who were searching for purpose, people who may benefit from joining the FA community and connecting with others.

I would meet people like Erin O'Neil who was diagnosed with

Friedreich's ataxia when she was twelve years old. Since she received her diagnosis in 1992, the FA community was almost nonexistent, the Internet was in its infancy, and she felt completely alone.

"When I was diagnosed," she says, "I didn't fully grasp what was going on. I asked questions as I went. There was no information. We had no support. I had no friends who had a similar experience. No one could help me plan for my future."

That future placed her in a wheelchair at twenty-one.

"The best way out of hardship is to help people out of suffering," Erin says. "The prescription to contradict the loneliness and isolation that comes with disease is to offer friendship. That's all it takes."

With Erin's words in mind, I felt empowered to continue riding in an effort to cast a wider net into the community. In 2010 I put together a team of four cyclists for Race Across America—"the world's toughest bike race."

Our goal was to ride all the way across the United States...this time in nine days.

RAAM Starting Point: *Oceanside, California*
Endpoint: *City Dock, Annapolis, Maryland*
Mileage: *3,005*
Total Climbing: *170,000 feet*
Time Allotment: *Nine Days*

Map data ©2018 Google via ridewithgps.com.

THE WORLD'S TOUGHEST BIKE RACE

I'm clipping into my pedals in Oceanside, California. Perfect waves beat behind me against the shore; surfers in board shorts spin 360s on symmetrical tubes and thousands of locals and vacationers lounge in the sand, while the din of 300 cyclists and a multitude of support teams fills the air—music, cheering, the whole deal—and I'm staring down the length of the pier, the symbolic starting line, about to embark on a 3,000-mile journey across the country in less than nine days.

The California coastal mountains rise to the northeast. Within the first seventy-five miles, we will ascend 4,000 feet, arrive at the infamous nine-mile descent nicknamed "The Glass Elevator," and then drop another 4,000 feet into the Anza-Borrego Desert.

Adding to the mix, we have a support crew of thirteen dedicated people, two follow cars, a six-man film crew documenting the race, an aging RV, and two media vehicles filled with coffee-infused young men—all to get our four-man relay team to the finish line at the city dock in Annapolis, Maryland.

In nine days.

Have I lost my friggin' mind?

Since my ride to Memphis, my balance and mobility have declined significantly. I can't walk unaided. I have transitioned to the wheelchair about half the time, and I'm anxious about the amount of physical stress on my legs, the potential damage, and how nine days of nonstop riding could ultimately affect my future mobility.

At this moment, however, the only thing that's occupying my attention is my foot. When I aim my cleat at the pedal, it slips out. I try to reattach my foot to the machine, and I miss the loop.

I could get sentimental and write that Friedreich's ataxia affects my spatial aim, but we've gone past that.

So what if it takes me a couple of minutes to button my shirt? So what if I must clutch, pivot, and plop in order to sit in my wheelchair? So what if I must use hand controls to drive a car? So what if I have to prop myself at the sink in order to wash a few dishes or ask someone to carry my cup of coffee to my desk?

What if there's no rising above anything?

After *rideATAXIA I*, I fully embraced the thought that a person is separate from their disease or disability. With this notion, we eliminate the curve, the norm, and the average range of ability.

So, we return to my foot. My feet aren't interested in equal rights, and they aren't amused by the triumph of the human spirit. They just want to get attached to my pedal.

After several attempts, I insert my foot into the loop and rock it back and forth. The mechanism stretches, connects, and clicks into place. Relief. I don't have to go anywhere for a while.

Have you ever seen one of those fully attired cyclists at a stop-light? The stubborn rider makes every effort to keep the bike upright, rocking the pedals, turning the handlebars back and forth, waiting for the light. That's because—with an upright—you have to unclip when you stop, and put your feet down. Of course, he has the option of falling over, which happens too often with the cyclist's feet still attached to the pedals. Not a pretty sight.

With a trike, since you're on three wheels, you never need to unclip. You sit and recline as if you own the universe.

And sitting on my new Catrike 700, I owned the universe.

The Catrike 700 is a beautiful machine, my dream trike. Easily —with its high-tech aluminum alloy and minimal weight—the fastest trike on Earth. The beauty of its design begins with the stiffness of its frame, which allows for a more efficient transfer of power from foot to pedal and all the way back to its rear wheel.

Behind my shoulder, the sun, inching past high noon, offers fuel to the scent of summer, rising off oceans, nearby canyons, and distant deserts. I'm intoxicated in the moment.

I glance to my left and right where my teammates Sean Baumstark, John Lockwood, and Mike Mellott are geared up on their upright bikes—all young men, pumped-up to ride for a cause that matters. We are wearing Team FARA jerseys with our sponsors emblazoned on the front and back. Around the collar are the words *Together we will cure FA*.

In front of me, the banner across the start line reads, Race Across America (RAAM), "the world's toughest bike race." I won't argue. It comes close.

During RAAM, in the team category, racers must traverse 3,005 miles across twelve states and climb over 170,000 vertical feet in less than nine days. To finish the race in time, the team rides twenty-four hours a day.

This is crazy, I'm thinking. I get that my clock ticks differently, but must it involve riding my trike across the United States night and day?

In order to stay in the running, our team had to reach Durango, Colorado—930 miles away—in 48 hours.

Before the ride, I maintained an active social-media profile, whipping my friends and loved ones into a cheerleading frenzy. I saw the finish line before we started, but there was no assumption that we'd make it. We had miles of horizontal and vertical feet to cover—a desert and several mountain ranges—plus heat, rain, and intense physical output. Hundreds of riders fail, as too much can happen between here and there.

We weren't going to fail.

LET'S GET IT DONE

After Memphis, a metaphorical tailwind pushed me forward.

During that first ride across most of the United States, I pulled the plug on my former life. I burned Old Self into the scorched deserts of the Southwest and the lowlands of the Gulf, and along the way I entered a community that was ripe for change.

When I completed my ride to Memphis, I wanted to capitalize on the momentum. I was thinking less about myself and my situation, more about how I could contribute to the bigger picture.

This perspective required a shift of presence. My involvement with the FA community and the support of my parents had pushed me in new directions. Love provided the engine to thrive, and my parents and the FA community helped me carve a path toward that goal.

Everyone had the same phrase on their lips: *Together We Will Cure FA.*

I committed to an alchemy that was not only grounded in science but in the growing conviction of this community. Sure, I had a great job and a strong career as an engineer. I even purchased a house. All I needed was a white picket fence. But when I began organizing for *rideATAXIA II* and again for *rideATAXIA III*, the cubicle no longer fit. I saw my career beyond engineer, a career I pursued because I knew it would add purpose to my life.

My old anxieties had not entirely disappeared. I experienced persistent self-doubt. And each time a member of my community passed away—young men and women who had become friends and teammates—the crushing sensation of survivor's guilt left me in tears.

I *had* to become a part of something that would insert me directly into the FA community where I could make a difference, and join the race to outpace the terrible effects of FA.

THE GENESIS OF *RIDEATAXIA*

rideATAXIA II was born somewhere between the Natchez Trace and Elvis's grave. At first, I just wanted another excuse to ride my trike, and a journey from Sacramento to Las Vegas seemed like a perfect opportunity.

Other people wanted to get involved and ride their bikes, too. So, I invited everyone to ride, whether they had FA or not. People were attracted to the rides, in part, because of the personal challenge, a way to confront their own self-perception. It was powerful to watch these transformations take place in the space of several hundred miles.

I didn't launch the rides with the mindset of thinking big. Too often, people assume successful organizations have a predetermined destiny. People think, *Oh, we can be like Google, or Patagonia, or Starbucks. We can launch a social media campaign, start a movement, and make a push to attract thousands.*

That's a fantasy.

During the ride from Sacramento to Las Vegas, we had a family friend with a pickup truck, who drove ahead and parked on the side of country roads, setting up food and water stations. At one point, a farmer who owned the property where our friend had set up a rest stop chased our retinue off his land. We were naïve and didn't know anything about permits.

We just wanted to make it happen.

That's the key. Grassroots development begins with one person and an idea, handshakes and hugs, and peanut butter sandwiches on the side of a country road.

A NON-STOP 24/7 RACE

After the ceremonial start in Oceanside, the RAAM team riders returned to their support vehicles, while leaving one rider on the road to continue into the California coastal foothills.

Our team consisted of four riders split into two sub-teams. John Lockwood and I rode on one while Sean Baumstark and Mike Mellot represented the other.

Sean was the second rider with FA on our team. He was diagnosed with Friedreich's ataxia when he was twenty-six years old, with 330 GAA repeats. Since he has fewer repeats, his body makes slightly more frataxin, which means the disease doesn't progress quite as aggressively.

After my first ride, the *Sacramento Bee* published an article about my cross-country trip. Sean saw the article two weeks after he was diagnosed. He contacted me immediately, which was impressive. Here's this guy, who gets diagnosed with a life-shortening disease and responds by saying, "All right, let's do this."

During the race, each sub-team rode continuously four-hour shifts. Each shift had thirty-minute ride intervals—known as a "pull"—where the guy on the road "pulls" the team while the second rider waits ahead to begin his own pull.

Meanwhile, the other sub-team drives three to four hours ahead to park and wait. To cover 350 to 500 miles a day, the relay team never sleeps more than four hours.

The entire experience was so volatile and unpredictable— anticipating the unknowns, dealing with nine people crammed into a six-person RV, sleeping head to toe—that at the beginning of the ride, I lay awake for two days, staring at the ceiling between four-hour shifts.

My first pull began twenty miles east of Oceanside.

I waited in the van for John to finish the very first pull of the race. I checked my helmet, adjusted my sunglasses. I had the same sensation when I was about to parachute out of a plane for the first time in Lodi, California. A friend with FA, Phillip Bennett, had planned a jump for his birthday and invited me along. I impressed upon him that I was ready for anything, but—between leaving the plane and free fall—those were the most terrifying three seconds of my life.

When I jumped from the plane, I tumbled toward the earth, not knowing up or down, strapped to the mercy of a complete stranger; it was a total surrender on a journey with an outcome I couldn't possibly determine.

Now, as I waited on the road to begin my pull, I was comforted by the notion of gravity. But I was about to "free fall" across the United States, a trip into the unknown—a challenge that would test the edges of my limits again.

Crew member Mike Andresen, who has two sons living with FA, pulled my trike off the rack and dropped it on the road about ten feet in front of the van. I pressed the button and the automatic door slid open, sucking in the dry, California air.

I stepped down, jerked around for balance, and found my footing. I was already unsteady on my feet, and my cycling shoes doubled the difficulty. I grabbed my dad's hands, and he walked me up and helped me sit down in the trike.

Someone gas-checked an eight-cylinder engine as they sped by, and revved the motor. I clipped my shoes into the pedals.

Ready.

I turned around.

No John.

Other riders passed. I adjusted my position, tightened the Velcro on my shoes. More riders passed.

No John.

Not that I was concerned. John was a strong cyclist, determined and focused, a serious sprinter with big piston legs. I was familiar with his cycling ability because he had joined us on *ride-ATAXIA II*. He understood the stakes of disease—his dad battled cancer to the end—but no matter what was happening, he was positive and upbeat.

Finally, the colors of his Team FARA jersey flashed near a bend in the foothills and my heart jumped. John was cranking uphill at an impressive pace—probably unnecessary—but he was standing over his pedals, leaning into every stroke. Oak trees arched above him, which kept him in the shade.

We had so much adrenaline. It pulsed in our hearts. At this point in the race, we weren't capable of holding back. Everyone hooted and John responded, pumping his fist.

My stomach fluttered, and as soon as John passed, I pressed down on the pedal. All my energy pumped into that first stroke. I felt the pressure of the ride, the anticipation of the unknown, and the miles looming ahead. Though I hadn't known it for long, I had been preparing for this moment for years.

I took off like a shot.

Our technical guy Steve Parsons (we called him MacGyver) had mounted a set of speakers behind the front grill of the follow van. The speakers were hooked up to a microphone so we could receive directions from the "navigator," who directed us to go right or left or inform us about a detour. The speaker was also hooked up to the car stereo.

As I cranked up the hill, someone slipped in a Proclaimers CD, and the speakers blared across the valley:

But I would walk 500 miles
And I would walk 500 more.
Just to be the man who walks a thousand miles
to fall down at your door.
The driving beat echoed off a nearby gulley.

And I rode 500 more.

PUSHING TO THE TOP O' THE ROCKIES

Someone shook me awake. It was dark. I groaned on the short and narrow bench in the dining nook of the RV.

Outside the windows, mountains surrounded the canyon where we parked beneath an immense sky. A small creek—the

South Fork of the Rio Grande (Yep, *that* Rio Grande)—ran along the road; sparse foliage grew low to the ground at the high altitude, where dawn pitted blue against snow peaked ridges.

I stepped outside, tightened my gear, and got ready for my pull. Crisp air and high altitude slowed my breathing. Headlights flickered in the distance from the other crew van as it worked down the pass. Soon, Mike appeared—red windbreaker, tights, full-finger gloves, hat to cover his ears. He was descending fast, leaning around every curve.

No. He was flying.

After reaching the highest point in the race (Wolf Creek Pass, over 10,000 feet) in the dark of that morning, Sean and Mike let loose on the downhill, reaching their top speeds for the entire race.

Mike was Sean's friend from church, soft-spoken, always upbeat. Upon first impression he appeared shy, but down a few layers he demonstrated a life force that could recharge anyone on the team. We all fed off each other. With his skinny, long frame, Mike was our climber. He didn't necessarily like climbing (neither did anyone else), but he was good at it, and we gladly volunteered him.

Durango was behind us. It was our most important qualifying marker. But when the opportunity arose, we wanted to defy time and push harder than necessary. This was a race against time, an elusive competitor that gave us the incentive to get in front of it. Or, at least, try.

The only problem: When one rider came down a mountain, another rider would have to go up.

As soon as Mike cleared my rear tire, I pushed off from the long shadows of the canyon. John and I relayed past farm land in a fertile valley near Alamosa, Colorado, and then up the switchbacks of Cucharas Pass at 3 mph—a walking pace. To mark the time, I focused on a tree in the near distance, five or ten minutes, pass it, and focus on another.

After our four-hour shift, we would descend from the Rockies onto the flat, big-skied, endless mirage of the American plains and lean toward the Atlantic.

It was only Day Three, but I had never experienced such pain. Press a finger into my leg and I'd scream. Trying to warm up and stretch was like coaxing an electric wire. I made mental scans of my body, trying to determine where I felt pain, wondering if the snags were worth any concern. I hoped I'd make the next pass.

After John started down the pass and hit the record speed for our team, 62.7 mph, I began my downhill pull. I was pumped from the beauty of the landscape, the crisp (and thin) air, and the knowledge that we were about to leave the Rockies and head into the Midwestern plains.

As soon as I took off, I overshot my speed on one of the first downhill corners.

When you're riding a recumbent on three wheels, you have to be careful on high-speed turns—any quick movement can flip your trike. So, when you're shooting down a 9,000-foot mountain, there's not much room for error. Every decision affects the trajectory of your rig. It's harder to see, harder to steer, and definitely harder to stop. Obstacles in the road arrive sooner than you think, and then you're off the edge of the cliff.

Within seconds, I hit 45 mph around another corner, and I was riding on two wheels instead of three. There's a fine line between being in control and out of control. I had crossed that line.

With my recumbent riding two wheels, I neared the edge of the canyon. I was moments away from pitching over a 500-foot cliff. Thinking fast, I corrected, and dropped my third wheel onto the road.

The sensation of that experience is familiar.

Whether I stumble toward love, race for a cure, or make a high-speed turn on a steep Colorado mountain road, I struggle to find balance in my life. Even the functional decisions continue to challenge me. For example, as my disease progressed, I resisted the idea of driving a car with hand controls. But what was the alternative? My legs no longer took orders from my brain, and it was only a matter of time before I missed the brake and drove into oncoming traffic, or off a mountain road.

I wanted to be in control of a body that had other plans.

But what does it matter if you're driving a car with your hands? The point of life is to get somewhere. It shouldn't matter how it happens, and that includes embracing any assistance—a walker, a wheelchair, or asking someone to hand you a cup from the top shelf—to complete everyday tasks.

As I have learned to temper my reactions to the changes that have caused me suffering, my life has begun to improve. I can make room in my head (and in my life) to direct productive energy toward things (and people and communities), where I can make a difference.

I can forget about planning so much for a "future" and learn how to effectively live "right now"; and I can throw myself into a community like rideATAXIA, which offers people a platform to approach FA from a place of pride rather than shame.

My life is no longer about me, but about us.

100 DAYS OF RAIN

(OR AT LEAST IT SEEMED LIKE IT)

We drove across the Colorado state line into Kansas in the middle of the night.

As soon as we hit the Midwest, the roads flattened and the landscape stretched into immensity. During the day, my eyes recoiled from the sheer distance. Even at night, with the moon overhead, I could watch the horizon, and allow my mind to wander.

Someone shouted and the transition from reverie to awareness was instantaneous. "Everybody get to the left side of the RV!"

A Midwestern wind slammed into us from the side, its force obliterating common sense. The RV felt like it wouldn't grip the asphalt. Dark green cornstalks carpeted the distance, as an oceanic wind-force silenced the surrounding landscape.

Eyes popped open. The RV rocked side to side. The muffled whine of the V8 filled the cabin. We fumbled with our gear. Nine people jammed into a six-person RV. Some slept on the floor, or head to toe, but we learned to move efficiently.

Lightning flashed, and then the rain started. Everybody groaned.

John was completing his pull, bending into the wind, gritting his teeth, gripping his handlebars. He was decked out in rain gear, but it was useless, everyone got soaked in those midwestern torrents. My pull was coming up, so I monitored a few texts to distract myself.

We had been posting our progress to the Team FARA blog. I received a text from Mark Bogucki, a Kansan and one of the first contributors to *rideATAXIA*. When Mark offered to pay one dollar per mile during *rideATAXIA I*, he inspired me to keep moving ahead. We remained connected, working toward a treatment and a cure for his daughter Lauren and the rest of the FA community.

With the wind and the rain now pelting the thin metal of the RV, I read Mark's text: *Welcome to Kansas, Dorothy. Ride like the wind. We've got a disease to cure.*

Mark's message made me teary-eyed—one of those moments of sentiment that connects me to purpose. Some days the pressure of my life overwhelmed me, the weight of our cause, the struggle in people's lives, the families on the line. This wasn't just a bike race. It was the execution of a dream. People like Mark reminded me that high stakes required perspective and humor.

I shared his text with the team, but no one spoke. A few heads nodded, but we were too absorbed with the intensity of the moment. I stared at their tired faces and I knew everyone shared the same urgency.

We've got a disease to cure.

The evolution of our community began in a hard place, with disparate sets of families facing a rare disease with no support, little information, and children dying a quiet death. With the discovery of the FA gene in the late 1990s, a small window opened.

That's when Ron Bartek and his wife Raychel stepped in to fill the void. Ron and Raychel formed FARA to build a unique research foundation that married patients and researchers to work toward a cure.

"The night our son had been diagnosed," Ron says, "Raychel and I sat down at the computer. We saw that there were isolated individuals around the world who had little hope because there was so little being done. I found a handful of scientists, no clinical trials. There was no basis for hope."

It was dark now, and outside my window, a flash of lightning and a barn appeared in the middle of another cornfield. I thought of Ron's well-known words: *Alone there's very little we can accomplish. Working together there's very little we will not accomplish.*

I measured the equation. Finding a cure to any disease contains every human feature, but its pursuit is troubled with intangibles. Elusive hope. Desire. Fear of failure. Small victories. Planning setbacks. Death. Still, the collective energy provokes activism.

When you enlist a sizable demographic that faces a seemingly hopeless set of circumstances, and you move them toward tangible action, an emotional wave accelerates the entire movement.

I became part of that movement, holding onto my handlebars. Ron and Raychel lost their son Keith to FA in 2010, six months before we left on our race across the country. As we pointed our bikes east, his life and death reminded us of our purpose.

In the thirteen years from the founding of FARA to RAAM, the organization had created strong bonds with numerous government organizations, built productive relationships with pharmaceutical companies and research facilities, while developing the largest patient registry for FA patients, ultimately providing a pathway to hope for thousands of people.

"We knew from the beginning that we couldn't do it ourselves," Ron said. "We had to build passionate consensus. We knew any other way wouldn't work. Every step of the way, we didn't accept confrontation. We thought: *This isn't competition. This is collaboration. It's a matter of the heart.*"

WATCH FOR THE POSSUM ON THE ROAD

I settled down for my pull at two in the morning. The emotional wave carried me into the rain. My heart carried me into the night. I felt exhilarated and focused. The finish line grew closer, but I still faced the intangible, that nagging infinity that visited me when I first received the diagnosis of Friedreich's ataxia.

We can all dwell upon end-of-life, our fragile relationship with our place on the planet, our weaknesses and shortcomings, or we can direct that energy with more precision: our ability to manage our reactions—how we treat one another, how we treat ourselves, how we interface with our web of relationships. These thoughts brought me back into focus. I pushed infinity aside and attended to the road ahead.

A gust of wind hit me. I ducked. More lightning flashed, illuminating more cornfields, followed by thunder. Before my pull, I zipped into a jacket and long rain pants, but it was useless.

Although my jacket was designed for ocean sailing, crazy wind, and inclement weather, the designers seemed to underestimate a Midwestern thunderstorm.

Since I didn't have a fender on my rear wheel, water sprayed up the back of my neck. My arms were mere inches from the two front wheels, and they received the next spray. With water spraying onto my forearms and face, neck and back, I had rain coming from four different directions. It took only five minutes for the rain to soak through my fancy gear.

I shrugged it off and pushed ahead in the darkness. I passed through an endless tunnel of night. Then lightning struck close, touching down in a nearby field, turning night into day. The landscape lit up for a second, which illuminated a barn next to the road. The obstruction blocked the wind for a moment and then revealed a wooden fence, leaning to one side that ran along the road for miles.

When I returned my focus to the road, a possum scuttled across my path, flashing his eyes.

I'm thinking, *I'm in his territory.*

I should be in bed.

But I'm not.

Each day, I'm driven by the notion that my life can get bigger and better. I'm driven to bring others along with me on that journey. I'm driven to understand how to make it work.

When I can empower myself to act, to prove circumstances wrong, even to prove myself wrong, I'm taking steps to challenge faulty perceptions of the "disabled" life.

Maybe "living bigger" means acting in the face of impossible circumstances. Maybe people perceive me as a "disadvantaged" person taking steps to overcome adversity. I view that as an opportunity to challenge ideas that define a limited perspective.

As long as we continue to move forward (and away) from our perceived deficits, then we're moving in the wrong direction. We need to move toward them, embrace them.

I strive to eliminate the need for *rideATAXIA*, to make my job at FARA obsolete, and to give thanks to the community of scientists, organizers, families, and individuals, in order to close the door on an FA-free world. After all, I'm in a business, which only has one goal: to go out of business.

But if this disease and disability must persist, while I'm able, I want to empower people to live a life without moderation.

RACE TO THE FINISH

About ten miles from the finish line at 1 AM, we were pulled over on the side of the road. At fifty miles out, all four of us had been on the road together, trading pulls.

Big leafy trees shook overhead. Weeds grew tall along the rural road. It was 80 degrees and humid, so we were in our jerseys and shorts. We just had to cover the distance to the City Dock in Annapolis, Maryland, and we had plenty of time to beat the clock, since we weren't racing against any other riders.

We were waiting for Sean, who was completing his pull, when a rider passed. It wasn't Sean. We recognized the team as the Aussie Oldies, a team of riders aged fifty and above who were riding fast. Their ride had stalled because they'd gotten a time penalty in Colorado.

We heard some chatter on the radio between our two vans. "Let's run this guy down," John said.

It was completely unnecessary, but everybody agreed.

With only a few miles left, we decided to lay the hammer down. John cranked away and rode hard for five miles, but didn't pass him. My dad, who had rallied for the cause, decided to put some fresh legs on the ground. We heard more radio chatter, and Mike sprinted ahead to catch the rider.

At some point, during Mike's pull, he passed the other rider. Then my dad dropped me on the road to finish the job. It was one of my fastest pulls of the entire race. As soon as I hit the ground, I started sprinting from five miles out. I powered through each pedal stroke, counting the revolutions until I reached the official finish line at a gas station located a few miles outside Annapolis, Maryland.

We reached the finish line in eight days, eight hours, and four-teen minutes.

Then on the last few miles, the four of us rode together as a team to the ceremonial finish at Annapolis City Dock. We passed people standing outside bars, smoking cigarettes, cheering us on. Before we passed the Aussie Oldies, the race organizers had already placed the team's name up on their banner with Velcro letters. When we rode around the last bend, the Aussie Oldies banner was still in place. I saw the confused expressions on their crew's faces, craning their necks, as someone quickly raised the Team FARA banner.

We came down the final chute and saw familiar faces, people in wheelchairs, family, and friends—about seventy people in all—who had traveled from across the country to stand at the finish line at 1:30 in the morning. We heard corks pop and saw champagne fly through the air.

Race organizers ushered our team onto the stage, where we were interviewed. I babbled on about the incredible support and love that surrounded us, but, most important, I talked about what defines a grassroots movement: people moving forward together.

Since that time more than 8,000 people have participated in *rideATAXIA*, with a total of $7 million raised for research, lives changed, and a community mobilized. Government, academic science, and big pharma have recognized that curing the defining features of FA may contribute to solving an entire host of diseases.

Thousands of families have been offered hope instead of despair, community instead of loneliness.

And it's all about a smile, a handshake, and peanut butter sandwiches on the side of the road.

Join us at a rideATAXIA event near you!

Find out more at *rideataxia.org*

Watch the award-winning documentary,
The Ataxian, about Kyle and Team FARA
in Race Across America.

theataxianmovie.com

ACKNOWLEDGMENTS

T*hank you to Coach Dory Willer* for getting me started and connecting me to the publishing world. This book never would have happened without you. "Trust your timing" was a piece of wisdom that guided me through times when it seemed like this project was stalling.

Thank you to Heather Burgett and Debra Englander for making the connection that changed everything for me.

Thank you to my agent Lisa Hagan for seeing the potential in my story and making it happen for me. Thank you for your continued strong support.

Thank you to the amazing folks at HCI and especially Allison Janse. The first thing you told me is that you wanted my voice to come through and I am grateful for the job you did.

Thank you to my friends and colleagues who put up with me when the book might have been the only thing I talked about for three years.

Thank you to Kele Dobrinski for the amazing cover design and for being one of my strongest supporters.

Thank you to Todd Palmer and Darren Price for the awesome cover photo.

Finally, a heart felt thank you to Alex Schnitzler for helping me understand what I was trying to say. I started seeing our phone calls as therapy sessions as you asked questions and dug deeper than I would have ever gone on my own. I am so grateful for the time you spent to understand and help me get it right.

ABOUT THE
AUTHOR

Kyle Bryant lives outside of Philadelphia, Pennsylvania. He is on staff at the Friedreich's Ataxia Research Alliance (FARA) where he is the founder and director of the rideATAXIA program, a series of bike rides raising funds and engaging the community for Friedreich's ataxia (FA) research.

When Kyle is not traveling to FA fundraisers, speaking engagements, and Rare Disease community events or recording in his podcast studio (storage closet in his apartment), you can find him on the bike trails of the Philadelphia area on his Catrike. *kyleabryant.com, @kyleabryant*

RESOURCES

Friedreich's Ataxia Research Alliance (FARA)

FARA's Mission is to marshal and focus the resources and relationships needed to cure FA by raising funds for research, promoting public awareness, and aligning scientists, patients, clinicians, government agencies, pharmaceutical companies and other organizations dedicated to curing FA and related diseases. *curefa.org*

rideATAXIA

With Kyle as the founder and director, the rideATAXIA program produces family friendly and personally challenging, single-day bike rides at locations across the USA and a few international locations with partner organizations. rideATAXIA welcomes people of all abilities to challenge themselves, connect with each other, and raise funds for FA research. Find your nearest location at *rideataxia.org*.

Two Disabled Dudes Podcast

With humor and insight, Kyle Bryant and Sean Baumstark talk about living life beyond circumstance and they interview people with similar ideals on their podcast. Guests include prominent figures in the rare disease advocacy community, successful disabled athletes and insightful professional speakers. *twodisableddudes.com*

The Ataxian

This award-winning feature length documentary tells the intimate story of Kyle and Team FARA and their journey across the U.S. by bike in eight days, eight hours and fourteen minutes. It consistently won the Audience Award for Best Documentary in the film festivals it entered. *theataxianmovie.com*

Cure FA Foundation

The Cure FA Foundation funds capital intensive projects gated with success milestones, leveraging novel tools of scientific research for the treatment and cure of Friedreich's Ataxia. *curefafoundation.org*

National Ataxia Foundation (NAF)

Patient advocacy organization providing support, education, and research funding for all Ataxias. *ataxia.org*

MDA

Nonprofit health agency dedicated to curing muscular dystrophy, ALS and related diseases by funding worldwide research. *mda.org*

Global Genes

Patient Advocacy organization working on behalf of all rare disease groups to connect, empower, and inspire the rare disease community. *globalgenes.org*

National Organization for Rare Disorders (NORD)

NORD, along with its more than 280 patient organization members, is committed to the identification, treatment, and cure of rare disorders through programs of education, advocacy, research, and patient services. *rarediseases.org*

EveryLife Foundation for Rare Diseases

Nonprofit dedicated to accelerating biotech innovation for rare disease treatments through science-driven public policy. *everylifefoundation.org*

Challenged Athletes Foundation

Through equipment grants and other programs, it is the mission of the Challenged Athletes Foundation (CAF) to provide opportunities and support to people with physical challenges, so they can pursue active lifestyles through physical fitness and competitive athletics. The Challenged Athletes Foundation believes that involvement in sports at any level increases self-esteem, encourages independence and enhances quality of life. *challengedathletes.org*

Catrike

Manufacturer of high performance recumbent trikes. *catrike.com*

Suiting up for battle in our tiny travel trailer.

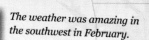

Riding through the Imperial Sand Dunes in the Anza-Borrego Desert with a bum knee.

The weather was amazing in the southwest in February.

An exciting border crossing.

Welcome to
NEW MEXICO
The Land of Enchantment

Not everyone wears pants in Arizona. Me and Paul, the owner of Reader's Oasis Books, in Quartzite.

We thought it was going to be all downhill from here. Not the case.

CAUTION
DUST STORMS
MAY EXIST

USE
EXTREME
CAUTION

ZERO
VISIBILITY
POSSIBLE

DO NOT
STOP IN
TRAVEL LANES

Okay, we get the idea!

The unassuming super-heroes in a Midland, Texas, machine shop.

The crank modification that saved the trip.

West Texas scenery.

Texas was good to us but it was time to go.

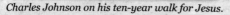

Charles Johnson on his ten-year walk for Jesus.

Louisiana's signature pear-shaped trees with moss hanging from every limb.

Mom and me.

The day before we reached Memphis. Perhaps my favorite picture of all time. Dad, me, and Uncle Steve.

At the finish line. We did it! Me, Uncle Steve, Dad, Mary Krill, Wally Krill, and Mom.

Team FARA at the finish line of the world's toughest bike race—Race Across America. John Lockwood, Sean Baumstark, me, and Mike Mellott.